CAMBRIDGE SCHOOL

Shakespeare

Julius Caesar

Edited by Timothy Seward

Series Editor: Rex Gibson
Director, Shakespeare and Schools Project

CAMBRIDGE
UNIVERSITY PRESS

Published by the Press Syndicate of the University of Cambridge
The Pitt Building, Trumpington Street, Cambridge CB2 1RP
40 West 20th Street, New York, NY 10011–4211, USA
10 Stamford Road, Oakleigh, Victoria 3166, Australia

First published 1992
Reprinted 1992

Printed in Great Britain at the University Press, Cambridge

British Library cataloguing in publication data
Shakespeare, William *1564–1616*
  Julius Caesar. – (Cambridge School Shakespeare).
  I. Title   II. Seward, Timothy
  822.33

Library of Congress cataloguing in publication data applied for

ISBN 0 521 40903 9 paperback

Design by Richard Morris
Picture research by Callie Kendall

To Elizabeth – who else?

Contents

List of characters   1

Before you begin the play   4

Julius Caesar   7

Julius Caesar – a play for every age   165

An alphabetical miscellany of Roman and
Elizabethan fact and fiction   169

William Shakespeare   183

Cambridge School Shakespeare

This edition of *Julius Caesar* is part of the *Cambridge School Shakespeare* series. Like every other play in the series, it has been specially prepared to help all students in schools and colleges.

This *Julius Caesar* aims to be different from other editions of the play. It invites you to bring the play to life in your classroom, hall or drama studio through enjoyable activities that will increase your understanding. Actors have created their different interpretations of the play over the centuries. Similarly, you are encouraged to make up your own mind about *Julius Caesar*, rather than having someone else's interpretation handed down to you.

Cambridge School Shakespeare does not offer you a cut down or simplified version of the play. This is Shakespeare's language, filled with imaginative possibilities. To help you explore all aspects of these possibilities, you will find on every left-hand page: a summary of the action, an explanation of unfamiliar words, a choice of activities on Shakespeare's language, characters and stories.

Between each act and in the pages at the end of the play, you will find notes, illustrations and activities. These will help to increase your understanding of the whole play.

There are a large number of activities to give you the widest choice to suit your own particular needs. Please don't think you have to do every one. Choose the activities that will help you most.

This edition will be of value to you whether you are studying for an examination, reading for pleasure, or thinking of putting on the play to entertain others. You can work on the activities on your own or in groups. Many of the activities suggest a particular group size, but don't be afraid to make up larger or smaller groups to suit your own purposes.

Although you are invited to treat *Julius Caesar* as a play, you don't need special dramatic or theatrical skills to do the activities. By choosing your activities, and by exploring and experimenting, you can make your own interpretations of Shakespeare's language, characters and stories. Whatever you do, remember that Shakespeare wrote his plays to be acted, watched and enjoyed.

Rex Gibson

This edition of *Julius Caesar* uses the text of the play established by Martin Spevack in *The New Cambridge Shakespeare*.

List of characters

Caesar and his supporters

JULIUS CAESAR
CALPURNIA his wife
MARK ANTONY
OCTAVIUS CAESAR } The ruling Triumvirate after Caesar's death
LEPIDUS

The conspirators against Caesar

Conspirators

BRUTUS	CASCA	CINNA	METELLUS CIMBER
CAIUS CASSIUS	DECIUS BRUTUS	TREBONIUS	CAIUS LIGARIUS

Family and followers

PORTIA Brutus' wife
LUCIUS Brutus' boy servant

VARRUS
PINDARUS Cassius' slave

CLAUDIO
LABEO*
FLAVIUS* } Personal followers of Brutus
CLITUS
STRATO
DARDANIUS

LUCILIUS
TITINIUS
MESSALA } Officers of Brutus and Cassius
YOUNG CATO
VOLUMNIUS
STATILIUS*

Other Romans

CICERO
PUBLIUS CIMBER
POPILLIUS LENA } Senators
OTHER SENATORS*

FLAVIUS
MURELLUS } Tribunes critical of Caesar

SOOTHSAYER
ARTEMIDORUS } Who try to warn Caesar

SERVANTS TO CAESAR, ANTONY AND OCTAVIUS

CINNA THE POET
A CYNIC POET
1ST, 2ND, 3RD, 4TH PLEBEIANS
CARPENTER
COBBLER
MESSENGER

1ST, 2ND, 3RD SOLDIERS

OTHER PLEBEIANS*

* non-speaking parts

I

Before you begin the play
The triumph of Pompey and Caesar, conquerors of the universe!

Imagine *Julius Caesar* set in a science fiction world. Here is how the return of Pompey and Caesar from their great expeditions of conquest might be reported:

> 'Last week Pompey, Caesar and their gallant band of cosmonauts returned from a voyage of conquest in outer space. They have brought back strange beings, monsters, artefacts crafted by alien intelligence and valuable minerals. We will see them all in the Triumph on the streets of Rome. Most of it is going to City investors. A 5000% profit to shareholders in the voyage!
>
> Excitement in Rome has never been greater. Children play with monster toys. They fight Pompey and Caesar's battles in the playground – against Mithridates, Tigranes, the Nervii, the Helvetii. Teenagers swoon over cosmonaut pin-ups. They go mad over extra-terrestrial fashion! Adults wonder at the City's new wealth – think what it can buy the people. Everyone is thinking: how can I get in with the men of the moment?'

1 Getting ready for a day at the Triumph (in groups of five)
Your family prepare for a day on the streets: packed lunch, cagoules, children to be got ready. Everyone is talking all the time about what they've heard and what they will see. Improvise the preparations!

2 At the Triumph (whole class)
You arrived late. You are all at the back of the crowd. But children can climb up high (on tables and chairs) and tell you about everything they see. Join in the cheering and shouting with everyone else. Welcome Pompey and Caesar back to Rome!

Pompey and the Senate! Caesar and the people!

(in groups A and B of four or five each)

There has been a terrible civil war. Pompey and Caesar – heroes always named in one breath – have fought each other for supreme power in Rome, and Caesar has won.

All of you are Romans after the war. Group A supports Pompey, who wants to rule more democratically, through the elected assembly of the Senate. Group B supports Caesar, who wants the direct personal rule of a dictator.

A A Pompeyite's point of view

'Pompey believed in the Senate. He fought for the Senate, he died for the Senate. One-person rule is dangerous – who's to stop Caesar becoming a tyrant? One ruler may serve us well, but what will happen when that person dies? Do we want all that superstitious nonsense about monarchs? We killed the last king we had 400 years ago!'

Make a list of the benefits of senatorial rule as you see it, at a time when there was no education for ordinary people.

B A Caesarite's point of view

'People in Rome are poor. Only the rich get votes in the Senate. Yes, the rich look after themselves. But with Caesar, you ask and you get. He listens and then he takes action – and he's richer than the Senate, because he's been off on his conquests again. Let him rule! Let him be a dictator! We need a strong man after the wars. But we'll never let him be king, of course.'

Make a list of the benefits of one-person rule as you see it, at a time when there was no education for ordinary people.

When you have made your lists, set out for Caesar's triumph. You either want to prevent it and make trouble, or cheer and enjoy yourselves. Improvise what happens when Pompeyites and Caesarites meet.

Two Senators ask a group of tradespeople why they take the day off work. A man who says he's a cobbler gives riddling replies.

---

1 Caesar's triumph, Pompey's defeat
(in groups A and B, of four or five each)

The Commoners are having fun. The Senators are smarting over Pompey's defeat. As players, find the difference of mood in lines 1–59 like this:

A Commoners

One of you try to keep a serious face while the group make you giggle. Move to the next player if they succeed or two minutes are up. Whoever makes people giggle most should play the cobbler, but everyone helps to make the lines as cheeky and funny as possible. Think particularly about how to put the Senators off through lines 31–59. Make it funny and you'll find the meaning will become clear.

B Senators

Think about the week's news and recall a distressing and sobering news item. Talk together about the feelings of a person who is closely involved, such as a victim or relative. In this way you can guess at how the Senators feel after the death of their hero, Pompey.

Divide the Senators' speeches between you, and practise reading them in ways that will show how you feel about the Commoners rejoicing at such a sad time.

When your groups are ready, join together and play lines 1–59 as a competition where your aim is to make the mood comic or serious.

2 Elizabethan humour

'be not out (of temper) with me; yet if you
be out (at heel or at your leather codpiece)
I can mend you,' says the cobbler.

Elizabethans were forever making jokes
about codpieces. The one in the picture is
comically large!

Look out for other plays on words such as
sole/soul (and cobbler, here, can mean a
person who plays with words).

Julius Caesar

ACT 1   SCENE 1
Rome   A street

Enter FLAVIUS, MURELLUS, *and certain* COMMONERS *over the stage*

FLAVIUS Hence! Home, you idle creatures, get you home!
           Is this a holiday? What, know you not,
           Being mechanical, you ought not walk
           Upon a labouring day without the sign
           Of your profession? Speak, what trade art thou?   5
CARPENTER Why, sir, a carpenter.
MURELLUS Where is thy leather apron and thy rule?
           What dost thou with thy best apparel on?
           You, sir, what trade are you?
COBBLER Truly, sir, in respect of a fine workman, I am but, as you would   10
    say, a cobbler.
MURELLUS But what trade art thou? Answer me directly.
COBBLER A trade, sir, that I hope I may use with a safe conscience, which
    is indeed, sir, a mender of bad soles.
FLAVIUS What trade, thou knave? Thou naughty knave, what trade?   15
COBBLER Nay, I beseech you, sir, be not out with me; yet if you be out, sir,
    I can mend you.
MURELLUS What mean'st thou by that? Mend me, thou saucy fellow?
COBBLER Why, sir, cobble you.
FLAVIUS Thou art a cobbler, art thou?   20

The tradespeople celebrate Caesar's triumph over Pompey. The Senators accuse them of ingratitude to Pompey, who was once the people's favourite.

---

1 Rhetorical questions (in groups of four or five)

Lines 31–51 make much use of rhetorical questions. Share the lines out making sure everyone has at least one rhetorical question. Practise speaking them, deciding where to speak harshly, where softly. Surround another group and deliver the lines. Then they do the same to your group. Talk together about the effect the lines have on the listeners.

Make a short speech of your own about a topical issue, using as many rhetorical questions as you can.

2 The power of Roman superstition (in groups of three)

Ordinary Romans were deeply superstitious. Every action or decision was taken after consultation of the augurers, who performed rites and sacrifices to find out the will of the gods. They were immensely powerful priests. (See **Superstition**, page 182.)

Deliver lines 52–9 as if you were magicians or priests with power over the people. Try different ways of speaking, and decide which one would have the most effect on the Commoners.

3 Modish mechanicals, stylish senators

Make notes or sketches of your costume ideas for the characters. Use clothing from any age.

---

awl tool for piercing leather
neat's leather cattle hide
tributaries conquered peoples
  forced to pay tax

Pompey see **Pompey**, page 180
intermit prevent
Tiber the river, sacred to Romans,
  that flows through Rome

COBBLER Truly, sir, all that I live by is with the awl. I meddle with no
tradesman's matters, nor women's matters; but withal I am indeed,
sir, a surgeon to old shoes: when they are in great danger I recover
them. As proper men as ever trod upon neat's leather have gone upon
my handiwork.   25

FLAVIUS But wherefore art not in thy shop today?
Why dost thou lead these men about the streets?

COBBLER Truly, sir, to wear out their shoes, to get myself into more work.
But indeed, sir, we make holiday to see Caesar and to rejoice in his
triumph.   30

MURELLUS Wherefore rejoice? What conquest brings he home?
What tributaries follow him to Rome
To grace in captive bonds his chariot wheels?
You blocks, you stones, you worse than senseless things!
O you hard hearts, you cruel men of Rome,   35
Knew you not Pompey? Many a time and oft
Have you climbed up to walls and battlements,
To towers and windows, yea, to chimney tops,
Your infants in your arms, and there have sat
The livelong day, with patient expectation,   40
To see great Pompey pass the streets of Rome.
And when you saw his chariot but appear
Have you not made an universal shout,
That Tiber trembled underneath her banks
To hear the replication of your sounds   45
Made in her concave shores?
And do you now put on your best attire?
And do you now cull out a holiday?
And do you now strew flowers in his way,
That comes in triumph over Pompey's blood?   50
Be gone!
Run to your houses, fall upon your knees,
Pray to the gods to intermit the plague
That needs must light on this ingratitude.

FLAVIUS Go, go, good countrymen, and for this fault   55
Assemble all the poor men of your sort,
Draw them to Tiber banks, and weep your tears
Into the channel till the lowest stream
Do kiss the most exalted shores of all.

Exeunt all the Commoners

The senators leave, intending to stop further celebration. Caesar comes to the Lupercal races where Antony runs. He orders Antony to touch Calpurnia in the race to cure her infertility.

1 Caesar's float (individually or in pairs)

Royalty in Shakespeare's day copied the Roman Triumph. They liked, on special occasions, to parade through the streets in a procession of elaborate floats like the one on pages 2 and 3.

Design a Lupercal float for Caesar, and other floats and triumphal archways, which emphasise his Triumph and the protection of Rome from evil.

2 A poem for the occasion

Queen Elizabeth I was often greeted at the gate of a stately home or a city with a poem written for the occasion. Write a poem to welcome Caesar to the games. Work on your own or in a group where each person contributes a verse.

3 Home from the Lupercal races
   (in groups A and B, of three or four each)

Group A is a coach party which breaks the journey home from the Lupercal races at a café outside Rome. Group B are the café owners who have never seen the races. Meet in the café and relive the whole event as you talk.

Scene 2 and the notes about the feast of Lupercal on page 176 will help to feed your imaginative improvisation. Also use your own memories of carnivals or festivities.

---

basest metal lowly spirit (with word-play on metal/mettle. Lead is the basest metal, inert but malleable)

disrobe the images pull decorations off the statues

the feast of Lupercal Festival held on 15 February to ward wolves off the flocks (see **Lupercal**, page 176)

stand you directly . . . sterile curse a Lupercal runner's touch was said to cure infertility

See where their basest metal be not moved: 60
They vanish tongue-tied in their guiltiness.
Go you down that way towards the Capitol,
This way will I. Disrobe the images
If you do find them decked with ceremonies.
MURELLUS May we do so?   65
          You know it is the feast of Lupercal.
FLAVIUS It is no matter; let no images
          Be hung with Caesar's trophies. I'll about
          And drive away the vulgar from the streets;
          So do you too, where you perceive them thick.   70
          These growing feathers plucked from Caesar's wing
          Will make him fly an ordinary pitch,
          Who else would soar above the view of men
          And keep us all in servile fearfulness.

                                              Exeunt

ACT 1   SCENE 2
Rome   A street

Enter CAESAR, ANTONY for the course, CALPURNIA, Portia, Decius,
Cicero, BRUTUS, CASSIUS, CASCA, a SOOTHSAYER, [a great crowd
        following]; after them Murellus and Flavius

CAESAR Calpurnia.
CASCA   Peace ho, Caesar speaks.
CAESAR   Calpurnia.
CALPURNIA Here, my lord.
CAESAR Stand you directly in Antonio's way
          When he doth run his course. Antonio.
ANTONY Caesar, my lord.   5
CAESAR Forget not in your speed, Antonio,
          To touch Calpurnia, for our elders say
          The barren, touchèd in this holy chase,
          Shake off their sterile curse.
ANTONY   I shall remember:
          When Caesar says, 'Do this', it is performed.   10

*Caesar is warned to beware the Ides of March. He dismisses the warning,
then leaves. Cassius remains with Brutus and accuses him of being
unfriendly, but Brutus says he is troubled by private problems.*

1 Caesar's progress (in groups of six to eight)

Plan Caesar's entrance and exit and how lines 1–24 can be staged. A
galaxy of choices faces you. How will you enact the stage direction at
the start of this scene? How serious is Caesar about the 'runner's
touch'? If he wants to be king he'll need an heir. How well can the
dialogue be heard by those on stage? Is there crowd noise?

Caesar leaves to the stately music of a Sennet. Music accompanies
his progress (Caesar says in line 16 that he can hear the Soothsayer
through it). What sort of person is the Soothsayer? How should the
great Caesar be seen talking to him?

Make your choices, then tape record or present your version of
lines 1–24.

2 A break in the progress of Caesar
(in groups of three or four)

Shakespeare wrote most of his plays in blank verse – lines of ten
syllables. Though shared between the Soothsayer and Caesar, line 18
is a regular blank verse line of ten syllables. Count them, then count
the syllables of other lines chosen at random.

Line 23 has only six syllables. These breaks often occur at
moments of crucial importance. Shakespeare's actor must pause for
four syllables (two 'beats') to think, to listen or to take action. How
will Caesar, all eyes on him, play this moment of silence? The Ides,
the fifteenth of the month, are during the full moon, an unlucky time.
No Roman will do business under the waning moon that follows.
Today is the Ides of February, so the Ides of March are a month away.

Play lines 18–24, taking it in turns to play Caesar. Think yourself
into his mind at this moment. When you come to play the pause at
line 23, hold a thought of Caesar's in your head that the others must
guess.

---

press crowd
Sennet formal, stately music played
  on wooden cornetts

soil discredit
construe interpret

CAESAR Set on, and leave no ceremony out.

SOOTHSAYER Caesar!

CAESAR Ha? Who calls?

CASCA Bid every noise be still – peace yet again!

CAESAR Who is it in the press that calls on me?   15
       I hear a tongue shriller than all the music
       Cry 'Caesar!' Speak, Caesar is turned to hear.

SOOTHSAYER Beware the Ides of March.

CAESAR   What man is that?

BRUTUS A soothsayer bids you beware the Ides of March.

CAESAR Set him before me, let me see his face.   20

CASSIUS Fellow, come from the throng, look upon Caesar.

CAESAR What say'st thou to me now? Speak once again.

SOOTHSAYER Beware the Ides of March.

CAESAR He is a dreamer, let us leave him. Pass.

              Sennet. Exeunt [all but] Brutus and Cassius

CASSIUS Will you go see the order of the course?   25

BRUTUS Not I.

CASSIUS I pray you, do.

BRUTUS I am not gamesome: I do lack some part
       Of that quick spirit that is in Antony.
       Let me not hinder, Cassius, your desires;   30
       I'll leave you.

CASSIUS Brutus, I do observe you now of late:
       I have not from your eyes that gentleness
       And show of love as I was wont to have.
       You bear too stubborn and too strange a hand   35
       Over your friend that loves you.

BRUTUS   Cassius,
       Be not deceived. If I have veiled my look
       I turn the trouble of my countenance
       Merely upon myself. Vexèd I am
       Of late with passions of some difference,   40
       Conceptions only proper to myself,
       Which give some soil, perhaps, to my behaviours.
       But let not therefore my good friends be grieved
       (Among which number, Cassius, be you one)
       Nor construe any further my neglect   45
       Than that poor Brutus, with himself at war,
       Forgets the shows of love to other men.

Cassius claims to help Brutus understand himself and the state of Rome.
Off-stage the crowd shouts. Brutus fears they want Caesar crowned.

---

1 Old schoolfriends in high places (in pairs)

Cassius is of Caesar's generation, in his early 50s. Brutus is in his early 40s. In Plutarch's *History of Rome*, Caesar gives Brutus a job Cassius wanted.

Think about a pair of students in your class. Imagine those two people stick together and, in thirty-five years' time, have formed a wealthy and influential partnership. Without realising it you apply for a job in their firm. They interview you but turn you down.

Improvise the conversation you have on the morning you receive the letter of rejection. Then talk together about Cassius' feelings towards Caesar and Brutus.

2 Traitors and loyalists (in groups of six)

Brutus makes a treasonable statement in lines 79–80 and puts himself in Cassius' power.

On slips of paper, write down six government jobs, put 'loyal' on two of them, nothing on another two and 'traitor' on the last two. Exchange slips with another group. Take one slip each, memorise it, then destroy it.

Improvise a party to celebrate ten years of a fictitious president's rule. Introduce yourselves and talk over the past, present and future of your government (make it all up!). In fifteen minutes, assess everybody's loyalty, but don't give your own away. Write your assessments down, then compare with other students' guesses.

3 Can you see your face? (in groups of four or five)

Some people worry about how they look to others; some do not. Try Cassius' question on unsuspecting friends. Report back on their responses and how a Cassius could use them, then guess at Cassius' thoughts in the long pause at line 54.

---

cogitations thoughts
jealous on suspicious of

a common laughter someone who
  tries to amuse everybody
  stale devalue

CASSIUS   Then, Brutus, I have much mistook your passion,
          By means whereof this breast of mine hath buried
          Thoughts of great value, worthy cogitations.
          Tell me, good Brutus, can you see your face?   50
BRUTUS   No, Cassius, for the eye sees not itself
          But by reflection, by some other things.
CASSIUS   'Tis just,
          And it is very much lamented, Brutus,   55
          That you have no such mirrors as will turn
          Your hidden worthiness into your eye
          That you might see your shadow. I have heard
          Where many of the best respect in Rome
          (Except immortal Caesar), speaking of Brutus   60
          And groaning underneath this age's yoke,
          Have wished that noble Brutus had his eyes.
BRUTUS   Into what dangers would you lead me, Cassius,
          That you would have me seek into myself
          For that which is not in me?   65
CASSIUS   Therefore, good Brutus, be prepared to hear.
          And since you know you cannot see yourself
          So well as by reflection, I, your glass,
          Will modestly discover to yourself
          That of yourself which you yet know not of.   70
          And be not jealous on me, gentle Brutus,
          Were I a common laughter, or did use
          To stale with ordinary oaths my love
          To every new protester. If you know
          That I do fawn on men and hug them hard   75
          And after scandal them, or if you know
          That I profess myself in banqueting
          To all the rout, then hold me dangerous.
                          Flourish and shout
BRUTUS   What means this shouting? I do fear the people
          Choose Caesar for their king.
CASSIUS   Ay, do you fear it?   80
          Then must I think you would not have it so.
BRUTUS   I would not, Cassius, yet I love him well.
          But wherefore do you hold me here so long?
          What is it that you would impart to me?

15

Brutus demands that Cassius come to the point. Cassius proclaims that no man of honour should submit to Caesar. He is a mortal but behaves as if he were a god.

Our great ancestor

Romans worshipped their ancestors. The more distinguished your ancestry the more was expected of you. Cassius reminds Brutus (line 158) that Brutus' ancestor rid Rome of the Tarquin kings and founded the 400-year-old Republic, now threatened by Caesar.

The Greeks, already ancient, claimed the gods as ancestors. Romans wished for a distinguished history so they claimed descent from the ancient and cultured city of Troy, destroyed by the Greeks. They believed that Aeneas, a refugee of Troy, recreated his native city in Italy and called it Rome. He escaped the flames of Troy with his ancestral images, his father Anchises and son Ascanius, all portrayed in this statue.

Ascanius' grandson, another Brutus, was reputed first king of the Britons – another people in search of its origins. So Britons could trace their ancestry right back to ancient Greece if they used a little imagination!

Ancestry to order
(in groups of three or four)

Newly rich Elizabethans wanted to claim noble ancestry. The College of Heralds could supply a pedigree and coat of arms for a fee. Shakespeare himself bought one for his father. Devise a pedigree and coat of arms for one of your group. Make them as fanciful as you can, perhaps using the known ancestry but only as a starting point.

---

outward favour external appearance

as lief rather

accoutred dressed

If it be aught toward the general good,   85
Set honour in one eye and death i'th'other
And I will look on both indifferently.
For let the gods so speed me as I love
The name of honour more than I fear death.
CASSIUS I know that virtue to be in you, Brutus,   90
As well as I do know your outward favour.
Well, honour is the subject of my story:
I cannot tell what you and other men
Think of this life, but for my single self
I had as lief not be as live to be   95
In awe of such a thing as I myself.
I was born free as Caesar, so were you;
We both have fed as well, and we can both
Endure the winter's cold as well as he.
For once, upon a raw and gusty day,   100
The troubled Tiber chafing with her shores,
Caesar said to me, 'Dar'st thou, Cassius, now
Leap in with me into this angry flood
And swim to yonder point?' Upon the word,
Accoutred as I was, I plungèd in   105
And bade him follow; so indeed he did.
The torrent roared, and we did buffet it
With lusty sinews, throwing it aside
And stemming it with hearts of controversy.
But ere we could arrive the point proposed,   110
Caesar cried, 'Help me, Cassius, or I sink!'
Ay, as Aeneas, our great ancestor,
Did from the flames of Troy upon his shoulder
The old Anchises bear, so from the waves of Tiber
Did I the tired Caesar. And this man   115
Is now become a god, and Cassius is
A wretched creature and must bend his body
If Caesar carelessly but nod on him.
He had a fever when he was in Spain,
And when the fit was on him I did mark   120
How he did shake. 'Tis true, this god did shake,
His coward lips did from their colour fly,

*Brutus thinks the off-stage shouts mean honours for Caesar. Cassius
mocks Caesar's greatness and tries to spur Brutus to action by
reminding him that his qualities rank equally with Caesar's.*

1 Greatness (whole class)

A visit by a popular and well-known person, especially royalty, creates
an expectant atmosphere. That person rivets everyone's attention.
Everybody smiles and laughs.

Recreate this atmosphere in your classroom. One person plays top
royalty on a visit, other students form his or her entourage. Plan the
visit together in some detail before you play it.

Afterwards, talk together in small groups about how your 'royal
visit' reflects Cassius' views in lines 92–161.

2 Cassius, the man on the public address system
(in groups of four or five)

a Queen Elizabeth said of herself 'I know I have the body of a weak
and feeble woman, but I have the heart and stomach of a king, and
of a king of England too'. Her femininity did not threaten the male
egos of her court when she asserted her authority.

Share ideas about what a 'real man' is. Identify Cassius' use of
'man/men' and explore his tone of voice in lines 135–61.

b Imagine Cassius' speech being given at a big political rally. His
voice is amplified through four big speakers one hundred metres
apart. Listeners hear the nearest speaker then 'echoes' from the
other three. Skill can turn this echo effect to advantage. Hitler and
Martin Luther King could make particular words and sounds
linger in the air.

Practise the 'PA-system' effect within your group, by cupping your
hands around your mouth. Then, placing each group member in a
corner of the room, read the speech continuously to the class, echoing
key phrases.

---

bear the palm carry the victor's
trophy
Colossus a huge statue of a god,
said to have bestrode the harbour
entrance at Rhodes

great flood the flood which Noah
survived
brooked tolerated

And that same eye whose bend doth awe the world
Did lose his lustre. I did hear him groan,
Ay, and that tongue of his that bade the Romans   125
Mark him and write his speeches in their books,
'Alas', it cried, 'give me some drink, Titinius',
As a sick girl. Ye gods, it doth amaze me
A man of such a feeble temper should
So get the start of the majestic world   130
And bear the palm alone.
                        Shout. Flourish
BRUTUS Another general shout!
I do believe that these applauses are
For some new honours that are heaped on Caesar.
CASSIUS Why, man, he doth bestride the narrow world   135
Like a Colossus, and we petty men
Walk under his huge legs and peep about
To find ourselves dishonourable graves.
Men at some time are masters of their fates:
The fault, dear Brutus, is not in our stars   140
But in ourselves, that we are underlings.
Brutus and Caesar: what should be in that 'Caesar'?
Why should that name be sounded more than yours?
Write them together, yours is as fair a name;
Sound them, it doth become the mouth as well;   145
Weigh them, it is as heavy; conjure with 'em,
'Brutus' will start a spirit as soon as 'Caesar'.
Now in the names of all the gods at once,
Upon what meat doth this our Caesar feed
That he is grown so great? Age, thou art shamed!   150
Rome, thou hast lost the breed of noble bloods!
When went there by an age since the great flood
But it was famed with more than with one man?
When could they say, till now, that talked of Rome,
That her wide walks encompassed but one man?   155
Now is it Rome indeed and room enough
When there is in it but one only man.
O, you and I have heard our fathers say
There was a Brutus once that would have brooked
Th'eternal devil to keep his state in Rome   160
As easily as a king.

Brutus says he will think about Cassius' words. Caesar returns, looking angry. He confides to Antony that he is suspicious of Cassius.

---

1 An aristocratic parents' evening (in groups of three)

To a true aristocrat, honour is more important than life, as Brutus has said at lines 85–9. He reinforces that view at lines 172–5.

Using Aristotle's description of the 'Magnanimous Man' as your assessment criteria (page 176), bring together the teacher and parents of young Cassius, then young Brutus, to discuss their progress in 'honour'. Make up their lives at home and school.

2 Caesar's secret police (in pairs)

Imagine that you are Caesar's intelligence agents who have shadowed Brutus and Cassius through lines 25–177 and bugged their conversation, in order to make a report on them to your master. Examine their words with care before you draw your conclusions. Also remember how they looked and acted as they spoke the most important parts of their conversation. Then make your report to Caesar.

3 Two newspaper photographs of Caesar's displeasure (whole class)

One half of your class arranges itself into a 'photograph' taken at the moment line 188 is spoken. The other half of the class shows the moment at line 195. Refer to the start of the scene for a list of the people in Caesar's train.

When your group has prepared your 'photograph', 'freeze' your pose while the other group tries to work out who is who.

---

meet appropriate
train attendants
Cicero great Republican orator (see page 174)

crossed opposed
well given friendly

BRUTUS   That you do love me, I am nothing jealous;
　　　　　What you would work me to, I have some aim.
　　　　　How I have thought of this, and of these times,
　　　　　I shall recount hereafter. For this present,　　　　165
　　　　　I would not (so with love I might entreat you)
　　　　　Be any further moved. What you have said
　　　　　I will consider; what you have to say
　　　　　I will with patience hear and find a time
　　　　　Both meet to hear and answer such high things.　　170
　　　　　Till then, my noble friend, chew upon this:
　　　　　Brutus had rather be a villager
　　　　　Than to repute himself a son of Rome
　　　　　Under these hard conditions as this time
　　　　　Is like to lay upon us.　　　　　　　　　　　　175
CASSIUS   I am glad that my weak words
　　　　　Have struck but thus much show of fire from Brutus.

Enter CAESAR *and his* TRAIN

BRUTUS   The games are done and Caesar is returning.
CASSIUS   As they pass by, pluck Casca by the sleeve
　　　　　And he will (after his sour fashion) tell you　　　180
　　　　　What hath proceeded worthy note today.
BRUTUS   I will do so. But look you, Cassius,
　　　　　The angry spot doth glow on Caesar's brow
　　　　　And all the rest look like a chidden train:
　　　　　Calpurnia's cheek is pale, and Cicero　　　　　185
　　　　　Looks with such ferret and such fiery eyes
　　　　　As we have seen him in the Capitol,
　　　　　Being crossed in conference by some senators.
CASSIUS   Casca will tell us what the matter is.
CAESAR   Antonio.　　　　　　　　　　　　　　　　190
ANTONY   Caesar.
CAESAR   Let me have men about me that are fat,
　　　　　Sleek-headed men and such as sleep a-nights.
　　　　　Yond Cassius has a lean and hungry look,
　　　　　He thinks too much: such men are dangerous.　　195
ANTONY   Fear him not, Caesar, he's not dangerous,
　　　　　He is a noble Roman and well given.

Caesar tells Antony that Cassius is restless, brooding and dangerous.
He then departs. Casca confides to Brutus and Cassius that Caesar
refused a crown three times at the races.

---

1 Entertaining Caesar (in groups of three)

You live in a distant province of the Roman Empire. Caesar is to
make a state visit and you want him to enjoy himself so your province
will get preferential treatment.

Choose four famous people from any time in history or the present
day to sit with Caesar at the banquet. Give reasons for your choice,
based on all you know of Caesar from the play. Find pictures of your
four famous people to make a wall display.

2 Cassius at home (in groups of four or five)

We later see Brutus and Caesar at home but never Cassius. Plutarch's
History tells us that he had a wife and a teenage son but gives no
further family details.

Write or improvise a modern day scene where Cassius and his
family entertain Casca at home. Make use of your knowledge of
Cassius, but add your own details. You can use current news topics to
keep the conversation going.

3 The author reveals all (in pairs)

When writing *Julius Caesar*, Shakespeare used a translation of the
Greek historian Plutarch. You will find the source of much of this
scene in an extract from Plutarch on page 180.

Together, one of you using page 180 the other using this scene,
identify as many of Shakespeare's alterations, additions and re-
arrangements as you can. Imagine one of you is an experienced
dramatist and the other a trainee dramatist keen to learn. Through
questions and answers come to some conclusions about why Shakespeare wrote it as he did. For example: why have Casca reporting the
refusal of the crown? Why didn't Shakespeare portray it on the stage?

CAESAR Would he were fatter! But I fear him not.
       Yet if my name were liable to fear
       I do not know the man I should avoid   200
       So soon as that spare Cassius. He reads much,
       He is a great observer, and he looks
       Quite through the deeds of men. He loves no plays,
       As thou dost, Antony, he hears no music;
       Seldom he smiles, and smiles in such a sort   205
       As if he mocked himself and scorned his spirit
       That could be moved to smile at any thing.
       Such men as he be never at heart's ease
       Whiles they behold a greater than themselves,
       And therefore are they very dangerous.   210
       I rather tell thee what is to be feared
       Than what I fear: for always I am Caesar.
       Come on my right hand, for this ear is deaf,
       And tell me truly what thou think'st of him.
                         Sennet. Exeunt Caesar and his train

CASCA You pulled me by the cloak, would you speak with me?   215
BRUTUS Ay, Casca, tell us what hath chanced today
       That Caesar looks so sad.
CASCA Why, you were with him, were you not?
BRUTUS I should not then ask, Casca, what had chanced.
CASCA Why, there was a crown offered him, and being offered him he put   220
    it by with the back of his hand thus, and then the people fell
    a-shouting.
BRUTUS What was the second noise for?
CASCA Why, for that too.
CASSIUS They shouted thrice; what was the last cry for?   225
CASCA Why, for that too.
BRUTUS Was the crown offered him thrice?
CASCA Ay, marry, was't, and he put it by thrice, every time gentler than
    other; and at every putting-by mine honest neighbours shouted.
CASSIUS Who offered him the crown?   230
CASCA Why, Antony.
BRUTUS Tell us the manner of it, gentle Casca.

*Casca says that Caesar had an epileptic fit after Antony offered him the
crown. After that, Caesar bared his throat for the crowd to cut.*

---

1 Life, death and honour (in groups of three)

Romans believed that to be honourable, you must hold life lightly:
'there are conditions on which life is not worth having', as Aristotle
says (**Magnanimous Man** extract, page 176). Cassius and other
major characters wilfully endanger or offer to give up their lives on
many occasions, as Caesar does here when he 'offered them his
throat to cut' or the mention of his leap into the Tiber (1.2.100).

Always question what characters really want on these occasions,
and what is revealed about their personalities. Explore your own
feelings about the value of life, death and honour in one of these
improvisations:

a a mother talks to her son about enlistment during a war
b mortally insulted by a superior fighter, you must decide whether
   you should fight a duel
c you are the family of a high ranking general whose country is
   minutes away from almost certain defeat. Should you use your
   cyanide capsules?

2 The crown thrice refused (whole class)

Study Casca's account. Then, with a Caesar and Mark Antony, act
out the incident in a leisurely way while two to three reporters take it
in turns to speak a running commentary into a tape recorder. The rest
of the class are the crowd in groups of three or four as families and
knots of friends who all have names and different occupations.
During and after the incident (which, of course, is punctuated by the
cheers of the crowd), the reporters can conduct interviews as they
move around, asking in particular for views about kingship. Antony's
account of his motives will be of special interest.

---

chopped chapped
swounded fainted

doublet Elizabethan jacket
man of any occupation tradesman
or man of action

CASCA I can as well be hanged as tell the manner of it. It was mere foolery, I did not mark it. I saw Mark Antony offer him a crown – yet 'twas not a crown neither, 'twas one of these coronets – and, as I told you, he put it by once; but for all that, to my thinking he would fain have had it. Then he offered it to him again; then he put it by again; but to my thinking he was very loath to lay his fingers off it. And then he offered it the third time; he put it the third time by, and still as he refused it, the rabblement hooted, and clapped their chopped hands, and threw up their sweaty nightcaps, and uttered such a deal of stinking breath because Caesar refused the crown that it had, almost, choked Caesar, for he swounded and fell down at it. And for mine own part I durst not laugh for fear of opening my lips and receiving the bad air. 235 240

CASSIUS But soft, I pray you; what, did Caesar swound? 245

CASCA He fell down in the market-place, and foamed at mouth, and was speechless.

BRUTUS 'Tis very like, he hath the falling sickness.

CASSIUS No, Caesar hath it not, but you, and I,
And honest Casca, we have the falling sickness. 250

CASCA I know not what you mean by that, but I am sure Caesar fell down. If the tag-rag people did not clap him and hiss him according as he pleased and displeased them, as they use to do the players in the theatre, I am no true man.

BRUTUS What said he when he came unto himself? 255

CASCA Marry, before he fell down, when he perceived the common herd was glad he refused the crown, he plucked me ope his doublet and offered them his throat to cut. And I had been a man of any occupation, if I would not have taken him at a word I would I might go to hell among the rogues. And so he fell. When he came to himself again, he said if he had done or said anything amiss, he desired their worships to think it was his infirmity. Three or four wenches where I stood cried, 'Alas, good soul', and forgave him with all their hearts. But there's no heed to be taken of them: if Caesar had stabbed their mothers they would have done no less. 260 265

BRUTUS And after that he came thus sad away?

CASCA Ay.

CASSIUS Did Cicero say anything?

CASCA Ay, he spoke Greek.

CASSIUS To what effect? 270

Julius Caesar

Cassius invites Casca to supper. Brutus invites Cassius to his house.
Cassius, alone, tells us he will use deception to turn Brutus against Caesar.

1 Conspirators as future rulers – the right stuff?
(in pairs or groups of three)

Old style Republicans educated their sons at home. Intellectuals like Cicero sent their sons to Athens. They knew the Greeks were culturally superior to the proud but uncultivated citizens of Rome.

At the time *Julius Caesar* was written, rich Elizabethans hotly debated where to educate boys. Should they keep them at home or send them away to the new public schools, rather than the local grammar school? There they would obtain a grounding in the new humanist learning from Europe, which included Latin and Greek literature. Some argued that gentry (high status persons) would be corrupted by mixing with inferior people any at school and should have home tutors.

a Judge where a person like Casca would fit into society today.
   Advertisers categorise us by 'consumer profiling'. Define Casca by the products he might use, the music he would listen to, the car he would drive, if he were alive today.
b Casca is introduced to Brutus as the sort of man Cassius wants to recruit for the conspiracy, but Brutus seems doubtful about him. Has the shrewd Cassius misjudged how they might get on together? There is a pause at 291 where Brutus weighs up what he knows of Casca with what Cassius has told him.
c Talk together about whether you believe it is best 'That noble minds keep ever with their likes'. Does mixing with other people corrupt or benefit those born with high status?

Conduct separate interviews with Brutus and Cassius about Casca as a potential conspirator.

---

tardy form slow outward appearance
honourable metal noble personality
meet appropriate

CASCA Nay, and I tell you that, I'll ne'er look you i'th'face again. But those that understood him smiled at one another and shook their heads; but for mine own part it was Greek to me. I could tell you more news too. Murellus and Flavius, for pulling scarves off Caesar's images, are put to silence. Fare you well. There was more foolery yet, if I could remember it.   275

CASSIUS Will you sup with me tonight, Casca?

CASCA No, I am promised forth.

CASSIUS Will you dine with me tomorrow?

CASCA Ay, if I be alive, and your mind hold, and your dinner worth the   280
eating.

CASSIUS Good, I will expect you.

CASCA Do so. Farewell both.   *Exit*

BRUTUS What a blunt fellow is this grown to be!
He was quick mettle when he went to school.   285

CASSIUS So is he now in execution
Of any bold or noble enterprise,
However he puts on this tardy form.
This rudeness is a sauce to his good wit,
Which gives men stomach to digest his words   290
With better appetite.

BRUTUS And so it is. For this time I will leave you.
Tomorrow if you please to speak with me,
I will come home to you; or if you will,
Come home to me and I will wait for you.   295

CASSIUS I will do so. Till then, think of the world.   *Exit Brutus*
Well, Brutus, thou art noble; yet I see
Thy honourable metal may be wrought
From that it is disposed. Therefore it is meet
That noble minds keep ever with their likes;   300
For who so firm that cannot be seduced?
Caesar doth bear me hard, but he loves Brutus.
If I were Brutus now and he were Cassius,
He should not humour me. I will this night,
In several hands, in at his windows throw,   305
As if they came from several citizens,
Writings, all tending to the great opinion
That Rome holds of his name, wherein obscurely
Caesar's ambition shall be glancèd at.
And after this let Caesar seat him sure,   310
For we will shake him, or worse days endure.   *Exit*

27

Casca meets Cicero and describes the natural and supernatural wonders he sees in the tempest which rages. Casca thinks they are bad omens.

1 All in a change of scene (in groups of five or six)

Shakespeare's scene changes can make very dramatic moments. They often highlight major themes of the plays.

Cast and act out the last two lines of 1.2 and the first four of 1.3 up to 'unfirm'. Three of you act, two provide sound effects; director optional. Note that Casca carries his sword (line 19).

Now imagine you were switching channels on television and this changing sequence is all you saw. Make a list of everything you might suppose about the characters, the situation, the circumstances of the action and the play as a whole.

2 The prodigies – a big production number!
(in groups of eight or more)

Combine speech, action and sound effects to present Casca's terrible visions in lines 15–32. Speak individually or together. Move around the room if you can to heighten the effect. In groups of three or four each take a short passage, you can learn it and be free of the script.

3 Prodigies on the wall (whole class in five groups)

Five prodigies are described by Casca. Imagine they took place in your neighbourhood, yesterday. For a wall display, each group should:

a report the prodigy, filled out with vivid details, interviews and comments from people you know
b Draw or paint it on a large sheet of paper
c As augurers (interpreters of signs) explain what the gods are telling the people in your neighbourhood through the prodigies.

---

rived split
sensible of feeling
against beside

prodigies wondrous sights
(interpreted as omens of the future)
portentous hugely important

ACT 1 SCENE 3
Rome A street Night

Thunder and lightning. Enter [from opposite sides] CASCA *and*
CICERO

CICERO Good even, Casca, brought you Caesar home?
          Why are you breathless, and why stare you so?
CASCA Are not you moved when all the sway of earth
          Shakes like a thing unfirm? O Cicero,
          I have seen tempests when the scolding winds   5
          Have rived the knotty oaks, and I have seen
          Th'ambitious ocean swell, and rage, and foam,
          To be exalted with the threatening clouds;
          But never till tonight, never till now,
          Did I go through a tempest dropping fire.   10
          Either there is a civil strife in heaven,
          Or else the world, too saucy with the gods,
          Incenses them to send destruction.
CICERO Why, saw you anything more wonderful?
CASCA A common slave – you know him well by sight –   15
          Held up his left hand, which did flame and burn
          Like twenty torches joined, and yet his hand,
          Not sensible of fire, remained unscorched.
          Besides – I ha' not since put up my sword –
          Against the Capitol I met a lion   20
          Who glazed upon me and went surly by
          Without annoying me. And there were drawn
          Upon a heap a hundred ghastly women,
          Transformèd with their fear, who swore they saw
          Men, all in fire, walk up and down the streets.   25
          And yesterday the bird of night did sit
          Even at noon-day upon the market-place,
          Hooting and shrieking. When these prodigies
          Do so conjointly meet let not men say,
          'These are their reasons, they are natural',   30
          For I believe they are portentous things
          Unto the climate that they point upon.

Julius Caesar

Cicero warns Casca that omens can be misinterpreted. Cassius enters,
bare-chested. He welcomes the tempest and despises Casca's fear.

---

1 Cicero Tours and Cassius Travelbreaks

While Cicero calmly goes home, Cassius seeks out the heart of the
tempest. Imagine Cicero and Cassius each run package tours. Plan
the words and images for their companies' television commercials or
the opening page of their brochures. The brochures should reflect
each man's personality and interests.

2 Entries in night and tempest (in groups of three or four)

Act out the entries of Cicero, Casca and Cassius and the three or four
lines that follow them. Talk together about why Shakespeare brought
them on in that manner.

Finally, choose any character you have met so far in the play. Walk
across the room in the manner your character would move through a
tempest. The group guesses which character you have chosen.

3 The world through Cassius' eyes (in pairs)

Read over the quickfire dialogue in lines 41–5 carefully, for meaning.
Hold an interview with Cassius as to why the night is pleasing 'to
honest men' and why those who find 'the earth so full of faults' find
the heavens menacing.

---

construe interpret
thus unbracèd with doublet
  undone

cross forked
from quality and kind depart
  from their true natures

CICERO Indeed, it is a strange-disposèd time.
          But men may construe things after their fashion
          Clean from the purpose of the things themselves.   35
          Comes Caesar to the Capitol tomorrow?
CASCA He doth, for he did bid Antonio
          Send word to you he would be there tomorrow.
CICERO Good night then, Casca. This disturbèd sky
          Is not to walk in.
CASCA   Farewell, Cicero.   40

                                        Exit Cicero

               Enter CASSIUS

CASSIUS Who's there?
CASCA   A Roman.
CASSIUS   Casca, by your voice.
CASCA Your ear is good. Cassius, what night is this!
CASSIUS A very pleasing night to honest men.
CASCA Who ever knew the heavens menace so?
CASSIUS Those that have known the earth so full of faults.   45
          For my part I have walked about the streets,
          Submitting me unto the perilous night,
          And, thus unbracèd, Casca, as you see,
          Have bared my bosom to the thunderstone;
          And when the cross blue lightning seemed to open   50
          The breast of heaven, I did present myself
          Even in the aim and very flash of it.
CASCA But wherefore did you so much tempt the heavens?
          It is the part of men to fear and tremble
          When the most mighty gods by tokens send   55
          Such dreadful heralds to astonish us.
CASSIUS You are dull, Casca, and those sparks of life
          That should be in a Roman you do want,
          Or else you use not. You look pale, and gaze,
          And put on fear, and cast yourself in wonder   60
          To see the strange impatience of the heavens.
          But if you would consider the true cause
          Why all these fires, why all these gliding ghosts,
          Why birds and beasts from quality and kind,
          Why old men, fools, and children calculate,   65

Julius Caesar

Cassius hints that the tempest is a warning that should rouse the people of Rome. Casca tells him that outside Italy, Caesar will be king. Death will free me from such oppression, riddles Cassius.

God gave the Ten Commandments to Moses in a storm on the mountain. When Moses returned his face shone so brightly he had to veil it in order not to blind people.

1 The voice of the tempest (in groups of four to six)

When Cassius talks to Casca, it is as if he reports what the tempest has told him.

Examine lines 62–111 carefully and work out the essence of what Cassius is saying. Then write or improvise a scene in which the tempest talks to him about Caesar, Rome and the strength of spirit. You could work it up into a magnificent presentation!

2 The power of Cassius' spirit (in groups of up to seven)

Working in pairs or groups of three, imagine that one of you has immense powers of control in your hands. By their movement, without speech, guide and control the movement of your subject(s). Swap roles.

Now, while two or three of you play the 'magician's control' game, the other members of the group divide lines 41–130 between them and speak them co-ordinated with the movement. Speakers and movers should inspire each other. Add sound effects when you are not speaking.

their ordinance their proper, required behaviour
thews muscles
yoke bondage, slavery
sufferance long suffering
bondman slave

Why all these things change from their ordinance,
Their natures, and preformèd faculties,
To monstrous quality – why, you shall find
That heaven hath infused them with these spirits
To make them instruments of fear, and warning   70
Unto some monstrous state.
Now could I, Casca, name to thee a man
Most like this dreadful night,
That thunders, lightens, opens graves, and roars
As doth the lion in the Capitol –   75
A man no mightier than thyself, or me,
In personal action, yet prodigious grown
And fearful, as these strange eruptions are.

CASCA   'Tis Caesar that you mean, is it not, Cassius?

CASSIUS   Let it be who it is, for Romans now   80
Have thews and limbs like to their ancestors'.
But, woe the while, our fathers' minds are dead
And we are governed with our mothers' spirits;
Our yoke and sufferance show us womanish.

CASCA   Indeed, they say the senators tomorrow   85
Mean to establish Caesar as a king,
And he shall wear his crown by sea and land,
In every place save here in Italy.

CASSIUS   I know where I will wear this dagger then:
Cassius from bondage will deliver Cassius.   90
Therein, ye gods, you make the weak most strong;
Therein, ye gods, you tyrants do defeat.
Nor stony tower, nor walls of beaten brass,
Nor airless dungeon, nor strong links of iron,
Can be retentive to the strength of spirit;   95
But life, being weary of these worldly bars,
Never lacks power to dismiss itself.
If I know this, know all the world besides,
That part of tyranny that I do bear
I can shake off at pleasure.
                              Thunder still

CASCA   So can I,   100
So every bondman in his own hand bears
The power to cancel his captivity.

Stung by Cassius' words, Casca commits himself to Caesar's overthrow. Cassius tells him of other conspirators he has recruited. One of them, Cinna, enters looking for Cassius.

1 I am a true Roman

Here is a verse about a slave:

I am a slave
I too had dignity once, but found peace at the whip's end
When I let dignity slip and be trampled by the chain gang.
I am a slave.

Read over 1.2.150–75 and this scene again, particularly lines 103–15. You will find that Cassius has a very clear idea of what a Roman should be. Now write a poem in the same form as 'I am a slave', but start and end each verse with 'I am a true Roman'.

2 Recruiting conspirators (in groups of five or six)

How did Cassius persuade other Romans to become conspirators to kill Caesar? Imagine that some conspirators meet to celebrate the anniversary of Caesar's assassination. They talk about how they were recruited. Brutus and Casca can give a detailed description (based on 1.2 and 1.3) of their feelings at the time, while Cassius explains how his methods were similar but different with the two men. Those playing other conspirators can make up the style and circumstance of their own recruitment.

---

hinds deer/slaves
bondman slave
fleering sneering
be factious for redress make a group of conspirators to set things right

Pompey's Porch Pompey's monument (in Plutarch's *History*, Caesar was assassinated here, not in the Senate House)
gait footsteps

CASSIUS And why should Caesar be a tyrant then?
        Poor man, I know he would not be a wolf
        But that he sees the Romans are but sheep;   105
        He were no lion, were not Romans hinds.
        Those that with haste will make a mighty fire
        Begin it with weak straws. What trash is Rome,
        What rubbish and what offal, when it serves
        For the base matter to illuminate   110
        So vile a thing as Caesar? But, O grief,
        Where hast thou led me? I perhaps speak this
        Before a willing bondman, then I know
        My answer must be made. But I am armed,
        And dangers are to me indifferent.   115
CASCA You speak to Casca, and to such a man
        That is no fleering tell-tale. Hold, my hand.
        Be factious for redress of all these griefs,
        And I will set this foot of mine as far
        As who goes farthest.
CASSIUS   There's a bargain made.   120
        Now know you, Casca, I have moved already
        Some certain of the noblest-minded Romans
        To undergo with me an enterprise
        Of honourable dangerous consequence.
        And I do know by this they stay for me   125
        In Pompey's Porch. For now, this fearful night,
        There is no stir or walking in the streets,
        And the complexion of the element
        In favour's like the work we have in hand,
        Most bloody, fiery, and most terrible.   130

Enter CINNA

CASCA Stand close a while, for here comes one in haste.
CASSIUS 'Tis Cinna, I do know him by his gait.
        He is a friend. Cinna, where haste you so?
CINNA To find out you. Who's that? Metellus Cimber?
CASSIUS No, it is Casca, one incorporate   135
        To our attempts. Am I not stayed for, Cinna?
CINNA I am glad on't. What a fearful night is this!
        There's two or three of us have seen strange sights.

Cassius orders Cinna to leave letters for Brutus in places where he will find them. Cassius says Brutus will join the conspirators tonight. They leave to join the other conspirators and go to Brutus' house.

1 Unspoken thoughts (in pairs)

Act out lines 131–43 with speed, but emphasise the pause at the start of line 140. Talk together about what is not said, but what is probably in the men's minds.

2 Conspirators in the night

Try to capture, in a picture or poem, the conspirators' frantic activity in the deserted streets of Rome. Use some or all of these vivid images from the play:

fire
spirit
tempest
blood
dagger

3 Facts are facts and books are books (in groups of six)

Shakespeare invented this scene. In Plutarch, there is only one paragraph of portents (which appear as lines 15–28) and no tempest. The story is not advanced at all by the scene.

Some people today do not like 'historical facts' to be changed when made into films. Similar people in Shakespeare's day objected to the liberties taken by dramatists. Shakespeare worked fast and often wrote or made changes in consultation with his actors. Imagine that his actors meet with a group of such objectors in a tavern after the first night and explain why their author inserted this scene.

Divide into two groups (actors and objectors). Prepare for the argument by listing justifications and objections for inventing or changing historical events in plays.

---

praetor chief justice
repair go

alchemy study of chemistry as a magical science, seeking to turn base metal into gold
conceited imagined

CASSIUS Am I not stayed for? Tell me.

CINNA   Yes, you are.
O Cassius, if you could   140
But win the noble Brutus to our party –

CASSIUS Be you content. Good Cinna, take this paper
And look you lay it in the praetor's chair,
Where Brutus may but find it; and throw this
In at his window; set this up with wax   145
Upon old Brutus' statue. All this done,
Repair to Pompey's Porch, where you shall find us.
Is Decius Brutus and Trebonius there?

CINNA All but Metellus Cimber, and he's gone
To seek you at your house. Well, I will hie,   150
And so bestow these papers as you bade me.

CASSIUS That done, repair to Pompey's Theatre.

                                                    Exit Cinna

Come, Casca, you and I will yet, ere day,
See Brutus at his house. Three parts of him
Is ours already, and the man entire   155
Upon the next encounter yields him ours.

CASCA O, he sits high in all the people's hearts,
And that which would appear offence in us
His countenance, like richest alchemy,
Will change to virtue and to worthiness.   160

CASSIUS Him and his worth and our great need of him
You have right well conceited. Let us go,
For it is after midnight, and ere day
We will awake him and be sure of him.

                                                    Exeunt

Night. In his orchard, Brutus sends Lucius to light his study. He decides that Caesar must die for his ambition to be king. Only death will prevent Caesar using his new power wrongly.

1 Scene changing (in groups of three or four)

On stage, voice and movement alone can show a change of place.

Cast yourselves as Cassius, Brutus and Lucius. Have a director (or sound effects person) if you wish. Work out how to change the scene from the storm-torn street to Brutus' orchard (from 1.3.164 to 2.1.9).

2 The divided self (in groups of three)

In the old morality plays of Shakespeare's childhood, good and bad angels used to stand either side of a character, persuading him to act virtuously or maliciously.

In lines 10–34, there are similar 'voices' persuading Brutus one way then another. Work out where each voice speaks, and where Brutus weighs up between them. Then act out the lines, giving each voice a definite 'character'.

3 Commonplaces (in groups of four or five)

Elizabethan schoolboys had to fill exercise books with commonplaces (line 21, 'common proof'). These were well-known sayings which they could use in essays. Sometimes they had to prove or disprove a commonplace. One way to do that was to build a story around it. Improvise a story around 'lowliness is young ambition's ladder'.

4 Make your own commonplace book

Begin your own 'commonplace book' of lines you enjoy in the play (see 3 above).

---

taper candle
general common good (general cause, as opposed to personal)
lowliness being respectful and pleasant to everybody

prevent act in anticipation
bear no colour for is not convincing

ACT 2   SCENE 1
Brutus' orchard   Night

Enter BRUTUS

BRUTUS What, Lucius, ho!
        I cannot by the progress of the stars
        Give guess how near to day. Lucius, I say!
        I would it were my fault to sleep so soundly.
        When, Lucius, when? Awake, I say! What, Lucius!   5

Enter LUCIUS

LUCIUS Called you, my lord?
BRUTUS Get me a taper in my study, Lucius.
        When it is lighted, come and call me here.
LUCIUS I will, my lord.   *Exit*
BRUTUS It must be by his death. And for my part   10
        I know no personal cause to spurn at him
        But for the general. He would be crowned:
        How that might change his nature, there's the question.
        It is the bright day that brings forth the adder
        And that craves wary walking. Crown him that,   15
        And then I grant we put a sting in him
        That at his will he may do danger with.
        Th'abuse of greatness is when it disjoins
        Remorse from power. And to speak truth of Caesar,
        I have not known when his affections swayed   20
        More than his reason. But 'tis a common proof
        That lowliness is young ambition's ladder,
        Whereto the climber-upward turns his face;
        But when he once attains the upmost round
        He then unto the ladder turns his back,   25
        Looks in the clouds, scorning the base degrees
        By which he did ascend. So Caesar may.
        Then lest he may, prevent. And since the quarrel
        Will bear no colour for the thing he is,
        Fashion it thus: that what he is, augmented,   30
        Would run to these and these extremities.

41

Lucius brings Brutus one of Cassius' letters. It strengthens Brutus' resolve to kill Caesar. Lucius reports that tomorrow is 15 March – the Ides of March.

1 Cryptic letters (in pairs)

It is usually hard to get politicians to listen. Giant letters, plastic babies, 100 metre strings of sausages – all these have been delivered to the homes of political leaders to make a point.

This letter gets Brutus' attention because it is puzzling or 'cryptic'. It is one among many ('such instigations'), all apparently by different writers but all in fact written by Cassius.

Write a cryptic letter to a leading politician of today about an important issue. Plan how to get it to him or her.

Help Cassius write two or three letters to Brutus, all prompting Brutus to action, but in different ways.

2 The Ides of March (in groups of three or four)

It is the eve of the Ides of March. There is a knock on the door. These things might or might not be significant to those on stage. Talk together about how you would stage lines 59–60 in the most dramatically effective manner and in particular how to make the knocking sound. Then stage your version.

Decide these things first:

Brutus and Lucius: Do the Ides of March mean anything to you? Any thoughts about the knock?

The Knocker: Which conspirator are you? Any thoughts as you knock?

See page 12 for the significance of the Ides of March to Romans.

---

flint flint with which to light the taper
exhalations meteors

Tarquin the Tarquins were the last kings of Rome, tyrants driven out by Junius Brutus in 509 BC. The Roman Republic then began. (See **Government**, page 174.)

And therefore think him as a serpent's egg
(Which, hatched, would as his kind grow mischievous)
And kill him in the shell.

Enter LUCIUS

LUCIUS   The taper burneth in your closet, sir.   35
Searching the window for a flint, I found
This paper, thus sealed up, and I am sure
It did not lie there when I went to bed.
Gives him the letter
BRUTUS   Get you to bed again, it is not day.
Is not tomorrow, boy, the Ides of March?   40
LUCIUS   I know not, sir.
BRUTUS   Look in the calendar and bring me word.
LUCIUS   I will, sir.   *Exit*
BRUTUS   The exhalations whizzing in the air
Give so much light that I may read by them.   45
Opens the letter and reads
'Brutus, thou sleep'st. Awake, and see thyself!
Shall Rome, etc. Speak, strike, redress!'
'Brutus, thou sleep'st. Awake!'
Such instigations have been often dropped
Where I have took them up.   50
'Shall Rome, etc.' Thus must I piece it out:
Shall Rome stand under one man's awe? What, Rome?
My ancestors did from the streets of Rome
The Tarquin drive when he was called a king.
'Speak, strike, redress!' Am I entreated   55
To speak and strike? O Rome, I make thee promise,
If the redress will follow, thou receivest
Thy full petition at the hand of Brutus.

Enter LUCIUS

LUCIUS   Sir, March is wasted fifteen days.
Knock within
BRUTUS   'Tis good. Go to the gate, somebody knocks.   60
[*Exit Lucius*]
Since Cassius first did whet me against Caesar
I have not slept.

Brutus describes how it feels to have made up one's mind to do a fearful act. Lucius reports the arrival of the disguised conspirators. Brutus muses that conspiracy must always hide its nature.

1 'The interim' (in pairs)

Brutus describes, in lines 63–9, a state of mind most of us go through when we've made our minds up to do an all-important act but have not physically done it. It could be facing up to someone we fear, or going to meet a life-threatening challenge, or changing our lives in a way that may have unpredictable consequences.

- Talk together about such times and how they make you feel. Improvise one of them, showing particularly what effect your state of mind has on those around you.
- Write a poem about Brutus or yourself, expanding his image of a troubled person as a kingdom in revolt.

2 Emblems

Justice is blindfolded and holds a sword and a pair of scales. Time has a long white beard, a scythe and an hour-glass. Such 'emblems' or 'figures' were very popular in Shakespeare's day. There were hundreds of pictures of them.

Study lines 77–85 carefully, then invent an emblem for Conspiracy.

You can draw it or write about it.

3 The Resistance (in groups of three or four)

Imagine your country has been taken over by an intolerable political regime. Your family have been approached by the underground resistance movement. You have agreed to a visit by members of the resistance organisation. The visit will change your lives. As you wait, you talk of how things were and will be, of your parents, your children . . .

---

genius and the mortal instruments spirit and body
mark of favour distinguishing characteristics

native semblance true appearance
Erebus the dark and gloomy route to Hades, the Roman Hell

Between the acting of a dreadful thing
And the first motion, all the interim is
Like a phantasma or a hideous dream. 65
The genius and the mortal instruments
Are then in council, and the state of a man,
Like to a little kingdom, suffers then
The nature of an insurrection.

Enter LUCIUS

LUCIUS Sir, 'tis your brother Cassius at the door, 70
Who doth desire to see you.
BRUTUS   Is he alone?
LUCIUS No, sir, there are mo with him.
BRUTUS   Do you know them?
LUCIUS No, sir, their hats are plucked about their ears
And half their faces buried in their cloaks,
That by no means I may discover them 75
By any mark of favour.
BRUTUS   Let 'em enter.

[*Exit Lucius*]

They are the faction. O conspiracy,
Sham'st thou to show thy dang'rous brow by night,
When evils are most free? O then by day
Where wilt thou find a cavern dark enough 80
To mask thy monstrous visage? Seek none, conspiracy,
Hide it in smiles and affability,
For if thou path, thy native semblance on,
Not Erebus itself were dim enough
To hide thee from prevention. 85

Enter the conspirators, CASSIUS, CASCA, DECIUS, CINNA, METELLUS, *and*
TREBONIUS

CASSIUS I think we are too bold upon your rest.
Good morrow, Brutus, do we trouble you?
BRUTUS I have been up this hour, awake all night.
Know I these men that come along with you?
CASSIUS Yes, every man of them; and no man here 90
But honours you, and every one doth wish

45

*Brutus is introduced to the conspirators. After some secret words with
Cassius he shakes their hands but he rejects the suggestion that they
should all swear an oath to kill Caesar.*

1 Will Brutus join us? (in pairs)

Talk together about what might be said in Brutus and Cassius' secret
conversation, then improvise it.

2 Dawn (in groups of three or four)

Julius Caesar was probably first performed at Shakespeare's Globe
Theatre on London's Bankside in 1599. The Globe stage was in the
south-west of an open circular building (like the Swan Theatre on
page 46). London's Capitol, the walled city with the Tower of
London, lay north and north-east (see London map, pages 172–3).
When Cassius dies, Titinius says 'The sun of Rome is set' (5.3.63).

Plot on paper the points of the compass. Then work out a staging of
lines 100–12 which will fill them with meaning for the first audiences
at the Globe.

3 Together at last! (in groups of three or four)

A documentary is being made about the Republican conspiracy,
twenty-five years after the event. Interview two surviving conspirators.
Ask them to relive the tense moments when Brutus and Cassius were
in conversation, then their coming forward together. Question the
conspirators on everything those moments meant to them.

4 Cassius' oath (in groups of three)

Cassius never gets to swear his resolution (line 113). Discuss what it
might have been and write it down (in not more than two lines). Each
group shares its version of Cassius' oath with the class. This will give
you many ideas about Cassius and the conspiracy.

---

fret cut ornamental patterns into
palter say one thing and mean
  another

46

You had but that opinion of yourself
Which every noble Roman bears of you.
This is Trebonius.
BRUTUS   He is welcome hither.
CASSIUS This, Decius Brutus.
BRUTUS   He is welcome too.   95
CASSIUS This, Casca; this, Cinna; and this, Metellus Cimber.
BRUTUS They are all welcome.
          What watchful cares do interpose themselves
          Betwixt your eyes and night?
CASSIUS Shall I entreat a word?   100
                    They whisper
DECIUS Here lies the east, doth not the day break here?
CASCA No.
CINNA O, pardon, sir, it doth, and yon grey lines
          That fret the clouds are messengers of day.
CASCA You shall confess that you are both deceived.   105
          Here, as I point my sword, the sun arises,
          Which is a great way growing on the south,
          Weighing the youthful season of the year.
          Some two months hence, up higher toward the north
          He first presents his fire, and the high east   110
          Stands, as the Capitol, directly here.
BRUTUS [*Advancing with Cassius*] Give me your hands all over, one by
          one.
CASSIUS And let us swear our resolution.
BRUTUS No, not an oath! If not the face of men,
          The sufferance of our souls, the time's abuse –   115
          If these be motives weak, break off betimes,
          And every man hence to his idle bed;
          So let high-sighted tyranny range on,
          Till each man drop by lottery. But if these
          (As I am sure they do) bear fire enough   120
          To kindle cowards and to steel with valour
          The melting spirits of women, then, countrymen,
          What need we any spur but our own cause
          To prick us to redress? What other bond
          Than secret Romans that have spoke the word   125
          And will not palter? And what other oath
          Than honesty to honesty engaged
          That this shall be or we will fall for it?

*No oaths – a Roman's promise is enough, says Brutus. He rejects
suggestions that Cicero be approached or Antony killed.*

1 Oath-taking denigrated and eulogised (in pairs)

Brutus claims in lines 129–40 that only bad, contemptible people
need oaths. Worthy people and good causes do not need them. In this
way he denigrates (condemns) oath-taking and eulogises (praises)
their cause. But every Elizabethan schoolboy knew from his rhetoric
lessons that, by the same technique, you could eulogise oath-taking
and denigrate any cause that was not bound by oath.

See if you can present Brutus with an argument that presents
oath-taking as necessary and desirable for all people.

2 Public relations (in groups of four or five)

Metellus sees (line 145) that the conspirators have a public image
problem, and so does Brutus (lines 162–83). In those lines, Brutus
shows the conspirators how to think of their task in a high-minded,
noble and honourable way. However, he does not show how to get the
general public to think of the assassination in the same way.

You are a public relations firm sympathetic to the Republican
cause. You have secretly been asked to prepare a 'package', using all
modern forms of media at your disposal, to give an immediate
explanation and justification of the assassination. Outline a PR
campaign which will convince everybody that Caesar's death is the
best thing for Rome. Provide such detail (posters, slogans, etc.) as you
think necessary.

---

cautelous cautious, crafty
carrions people who are half dead

insuppressive mettle irrepressible
nature
no whit not at all

Swear priests and cowards and men cautelous,
Old feeble carrions, and such suffering souls   130
That welcome wrongs: unto bad causes swear
Such creatures as men doubt. But do not stain
The even virtue of our enterprise,
Nor th'insuppressive mettle of our spirits,
To think that or our cause or our performance   135
Did need an oath, when every drop of blood
That every Roman bears, and nobly bears,
Is guilty of a several bastardy
If he do break the smallest particle
Of any promise that hath passed from him.   140

CASSIUS But what of Cicero? Shall we sound him?
       I think he will stand very strong with us.

CASCA Let us not leave him out.

CINNA   No, by no means.

METELLUS O, let us have him, for his silver hairs
       Will purchase us a good opinion   145
       And buy men's voices to commend our deeds.
       It shall be said his judgement ruled our hands;
       Our youths and wildness shall no whit appear,
       But all be buried in his gravity.

BRUTUS O, name him not, let us not break with him,   150
       For he will never follow anything
       That other men begin.

CASSIUS   Then leave him out.

CASCA Indeed he is not fit.

DECIUS Shall no man else be touched but only Caesar?

CASSIUS Decius, well urged. I think it is not meet   155
       Mark Antony, so well beloved of Caesar,
       Should outlive Caesar. We shall find of him
       A shrewd contriver. And, you know, his means,
       If he improve them, may well stretch so far
       As to annoy us all, which to prevent,   160
       Let Antony and Caesar fall together.

BRUTUS Our course will seem too bloody, Caius Cassius,
       To cut the head off and then hack the limbs –
       Like wrath in death and envy afterwards –
       For Antony is but a limb of Caesar.   165

Brutus says Caesar must be killed, not with spite, but with regret. Again, he overrules Cassius' fears about Antony. Cassius worries that superstition may keep Caesar at home.

1 The sacrifice of Caesar (in groups of three or four)

'Let's be sacrificers, but not butchers', says Brutus.

Firstly, mime the difference between butchering an animal and sacrificing it? In the Bible, Leviticus has detailed rites. See also **Sacrifice**, page 181. Talk together about whether it is possible to 'sacrifice' an unsuspecting human going about his or her daily business, perhaps illustrating your ideas with actions. Then read again Brutus' words (lines 166–80) and weigh them up carefully.

2 Why should Antony die? (in pairs)

Brutus interrupts Cassius at line 185 and the clock ends that discussion at line 192.

Have the clock strike later in order to let Cassius voice his shrewdest suspicions about Antony and his friendship with Caesar. He could change the course of history!

3 Conspirators caught in conspiracy
(in pairs or groups of three)

Imagine Caesar's agents, with or without Caesar's knowledge, have bugged Brutus' house. Now, with cast-iron proof of conspiracy, they arrest the conspirators.

Construct a case for their defence. 'Diminished responsibility due to freak weather conditions' is a possible plea, sometimes used in Mediterranean countries where odd climatic conditions are thought to unbalance the mind. See if the evidence supports it.

---

augurers a group of state officers who decided whether it was lucky or unlucky to undertake business on a particular day. Caesar had been an augurer (see **Superstition**, page 182 for more details)

Let's be sacrificers, but not butchers, Caius.
We all stand up against the spirit of Caesar,
And in the spirit of men there is no blood.
O, that we then could come by Caesar's spirit
And not dismember Caesar! But, alas,   170
Caesar must bleed for it. And, gentle friends,
Let's kill him boldly, but not wrathfully;
Let's carve him as a dish fit for the gods,
Not hew him as a carcass fit for hounds.
And let our hearts, as subtle masters do,   175
Stir up their servants to an act of rage
And after seem to chide 'em. This shall make
Our purpose necessary, and not envious;
Which so appearing to the common eyes,
We shall be called purgers, not murderers.   180
And for Mark Antony, think not of him,
For he can do no more than Caesar's arm
When Caesar's head is off.
CASSIUS   Yet I fear him,
For in the engrafted love he bears to Caesar –
BRUTUS Alas, good Cassius, do not think of him.   185
If he love Caesar, all that he can do
Is to himself – take thought and die for Caesar;
And that were much he should, for he is given
To sports, to wildness, and much company.
TREBONIUS There is no fear in him, let him not die,   190
For he will live and laugh at this hereafter.
                        Clock strikes
BRUTUS Peace, count the clock.
CASSIUS   The clock hath stricken three.
TREBONIUS 'Tis time to part.
CASSIUS   But it is doubtful yet
Whether Caesar will come forth today or no,
For he is superstitious grown of late,   195
Quite from the main opinion he held once
Of fantasy, of dreams, and ceremonies.
It may be these apparent prodigies,
The unaccustomed terror of this night,
And the persuasion of his augurers   200
May hold him from the Capitol today.

Decius says he'll bring Caesar to the Capitol. The conspirators agree to
meet at 8.00 a.m. at Caesar's house. They leave Brutus alone. Portia
enters and Brutus questions why she has risen.

1 To catch a toad with a wellington boot (in pairs)

Geffrey Whitney's *A Choice of*
Emblems (1586) shows how to
catch an elephant. Thought to
have no knee joints, it was
believed that they slept leaning
on trees. If you weakened the
tree beforehand, it would
collapse and the elephant would
be unable to get up.

Explain to each other exactly
how you catch animals by the
methods outlined in lines 204–6. Help Decius devise even more
absurd superstitions. Write down the best.

2 Brutus, in with us at last! (in groups of three)

The last eight lines of 1.3 showed how much Cassius and Casca
wanted Brutus to join the conspiracy. Brutus has now joined.

Hold a conversation between three other conspirators, keyed up
about tomorrow, as they walk away from the meeting. They assess
how the meeting went and whether Brutus' membership has already
changed things, for better or worse.

3 Lucius' dream

Write Lucius' dream as he slept through the meeting of the
conspirators.

---

toils nets
his humour the way he thinks and
  feels

DECIUS Never fear that. If he be so resolved
        I can o'ersway him, for he loves to hear
        That unicorns may be betrayed with trees,
        And bears with glasses, elephants with holes,   205
        Lions with toils, and men with flatterers.
        But when I tell him he hates flatterers
        He says he does, being then most flatterèd.
        Let me work:
        For I can give his humour the true bent,   210
        And I will bring him to the Capitol.
CASSIUS Nay, we will all of us be there to fetch him.
BRUTUS By the eighth hour, is that the uttermost?
CINNA Be that the uttermost, and fail not then.
METELLUS Caius Ligarius doth bear Caesar hard,   215
        Who rated him for speaking well of Pompey.
        I wonder none of you have thought of him.
BRUTUS Now, good Metellus, go along by him.
        He loves me well, and I have given him reasons.
        Send him but hither and I'll fashion him.   220
CASSIUS The morning comes upon's. We'll leave you, Brutus,
        And, friends, disperse yourselves, but all remember
        What you have said and show yourselves true Romans.
BRUTUS Good gentlemen, look fresh and merrily:
        Let not our looks put on our purposes,   225
        But bear it as our Roman actors do,
        With untired spirits and formal constancy.
        And so good morrow to you every one.

                                    Exeunt [all but] Brutus

        Boy! Lucius! Fast asleep? It is no matter,
        Enjoy the honey-heavy dew of slumber.   230
        Thou hast no figures nor no fantasies
        Which busy care draws in the brains of men,
        Therefore thou sleep'st so sound.

                        Enter PORTIA

PORTIA   Brutus, my lord.
BRUTUS Portia! What mean you? Wherefore rise you now?
        It is not for your health thus to commit   235
        Your weak condition to the raw cold morning.

Portia tells Brutus how difficult he has been since yesterday. He tells her he's sick. Then why is he out of bed? she asks, insisting on the truth.

1 An uncurtained window (in groups of three or four)

As one or two of you read lines 238–51 ('yesternight'), action by action, pausing after each, two of you act out the scene without sound, as you might see it through an uncurtained window.

2 What's on Brutus' mind? (in groups of four or five)

Brutus says very little to Portia. His mind is probably on the assassination. Gather speeches by Brutus and others about the assassination (1.2.92–161, 2.1.10–34 and 154–91). Then, while two of you read this part of the scene as Brutus and Portia, the rest of you urgently speak the gathered speeches into Brutus' ear, like Brutus' turbulent thoughts. Brutus' thoughts vie with Portia as hard as possible, without physical action or raised voices, to get Brutus' undivided attention.

Afterwards, Brutus can tell you what got through and what it felt like to have so much on his mind.

3 'Upon my knees' (in pairs)

Improvise a situation in which somebody you look up to and respect kneels to ask something of you. That somebody could be a parent, a teacher or someone you admire on television. It is an important matter, not a joke. Discuss how this makes both of you feel.

Now read aloud Portia's plea from line 266 to Brutus' reply, and work out what is happening between them here.

---

physical medically advisable
unbracèd with clothes unfastened

humours unhealthy moisture
rheumy moist and catarrhal

PORTIA Nor for yours neither. Y'have ungently, Brutus,
Stole from my bed; and yesternight at supper
You suddenly arose and walked about,
Musing and sighing, with your arms across,   240
And when I asked you what the matter was,
You stared upon me with ungentle looks.
I urged you further, then you scratched your head
And too impatiently stamped with your foot.
Yet I insisted, yet you answered not,   245
But with an angry wafture of your hand
Gave sign for me to leave you. So I did,
Fearing to strengthen that impatience
Which seemed too much enkindled, and withal
Hoping it was but an effect of humour   250
Which sometime hath his hour with every man.
It will not let you eat nor talk nor sleep;
And could it work so much upon your shape
As it hath much prevailed on your condition,
I should not know you, Brutus. Dear my lord,   255
Make me acquainted with your cause of grief.
BRUTUS I am not well in health, and that is all.
PORTIA Brutus is wise, and were he not in health
He would embrace the means to come by it.
BRUTUS Why, so I do. Good Portia, go to bed.   260
PORTIA Is Brutus sick? And is it physical
To walk unbracèd and suck up the humours
Of the dank morning? What, is Brutus sick?
And will he steal out of his wholesome bed
To dare the vile contagion of the night   265
And tempt the rheumy and unpurgèd air
To add unto his sickness? No, my Brutus,
You have some sick offence within your mind,
Which by the right and virtue of my place
I ought to know of. And upon my knees   270
I charm you, by my once commended beauty,
By all your vows of love, and that great vow
Which did incorporate and make us one,
That you unfold to me, your self, your half,

You exclude me, claims Portia – who were those visitors? She reveals a terrible wound, self-inflicted to show him her courage, secrecy and love. Brutus is moved.

1 Portia's wound (in groups of four or five)

You are all Portia, in the moments before she inflicts the wound on her thigh. Why did she do it?

Sit in a circle, each holding an imaginary knife. In turn, speak the thoughts that lead up to your 'voluntary wound'. When you feel ready to inflict the wound, bring the knife down violently on your thigh. Those who have not brought the knife down should continue speaking until they do feel ready. When everyone has brought their knife down, talk together about Portia's reasons.

2 Brutus tells all (in pairs)

Later (2.4.9), it seems that Brutus did tell Portia the reasons for his behaviour. Improvise the scene in which he explains all. Portia would probably not let anything go unquestioned. She may well have comments and insights about everybody involved, conspirators and Caesarites alike.

3 Brutus and Portia – a private glimpse
(in groups of three or four)

Imagine you write for a popular magazine. Your editor has asked you to 'profile' Brutus and Portia, to give your readers a flavour of their home and their life together.

Prepare by reading lines 1–60, as well as lines 229–309. Remember the reputation Brutus has built up through the play so far. An improvised interview with them could fill out your 'copy'. Include pictures if possible.

---

in sort or limitation after a fashion or within strict limits
Cato's daughter Portia's father and grandfather were famous die-hard Republicans (see page 171 for more details)

engagements dealings
construe interpret, tell

Why you are heavy and what men tonight   275
Have had resort to you, for here have been
Some six or seven who did hide their faces
Even from darkness.
BRUTUS   Kneel not, gentle Portia.
PORTIA I should not need if you were gentle Brutus.
Within the bond of marriage, tell me, Brutus,   280
Is it excepted I should know no secrets
That appertain to you? Am I your self
But, as it were, in sort or limitation,
To keep with you at meals, comfort your bed,
And talk to you sometimes? Dwell I but in the suburbs   285
Of your good pleasure? If it be no more
Portia is Brutus' harlot, not his wife.
BRUTUS You are my true and honourable wife,
As dear to me as are the ruddy drops
That visit my sad heart.   290
PORTIA If this were true, then should I know this secret.
I grant I am a woman, but withal
A woman that Lord Brutus took to wife.
I grant I am a woman, but withal
A woman well reputed, Cato's daughter.   295
Think you I am no stronger than my sex,
Being so fathered and so husbanded?
Tell me your counsels, I will not disclose 'em.
I have made strong proof of my constancy,
Giving myself a voluntary wound   300
Here, in the thigh. Can I bear that with patience
And not my husband's secrets?
BRUTUS   O ye gods,
Render me worthy of this noble wife!
                              Knock
Hark, hark, one knocks. Portia, go in a while,
And by and by thy bosom shall partake   305
The secrets of my heart.
All my engagements I will construe to thee,
All the charactery of my sad brows.
Leave me with haste.
                                                    Exit Portia
Lucius, who's that knocks?

The sick Ligarius enters. Brutus asks for his help. Ligarius recovers and swears blind obedience to Brutus.

---

1 The miraculous healing of Ligarius?

Write Ligarius' experience as a story or poem. You can do this on your own or in a group, writing a scene each. Possible scenes are:

- sick in bed
- Metellus' visit
- hurrying through turbulent Roman streets, mind racing
- arriving, seeing Brutus
- being asked to help
- how he feels after he leaves Brutus.

You can write in the first person (I) as Ligarius or third person (he). Help the reader to relive Ligarius' night in vivid detail. His senses are unusually heightened as in a fever ('Sick Boy' in Laurie Lee's *Cider with Rosie* describes this well). Try to convey everything that Brutus means to his admirers.

2 Lucius' night (in groups of three or four)

Lucius probably knows as little as Portia about the conspirators but has watched their coming and going. He must have sensed an atmosphere, seen expressions on faces, observed how people move and carry themselves, heard the tone of their voices.

Improvise a conversation Lucius holds with the other slaves next morning, describing that night. The slaves ask many questions and have plenty of ideas about what it all means. They may get it right – or they may not!

Enter LUCIUS *and* LIGARIUS

LUCIUS Here is a sick man that would speak with you.   310
BRUTUS Caius Ligarius, that Metellus spake of.
    Boy, stand aside.

                                                [*Exit Lucius*]

              Caius Ligarius, how?
LIGARIUS Vouchsafe good morrow from a feeble tongue.
BRUTUS O, what a time have you chose out, brave Caius,
    To wear a kerchief! Would you were not sick!   315
LIGARIUS I am not sick if Brutus have in hand
    Any exploit worthy the name of honour.
BRUTUS Such an exploit have I in hand, Ligarius,
    Had you a healthful ear to hear of it.
LIGARIUS By all the gods that Romans bow before,   320
    I here discard my sickness!
              [*He pulls off his kerchief*]
                    Soul of Rome,
    Brave son, derived from honourable loins,
    Thou, like an exorcist, hast conjured up
    My mortifièd spirit. Now bid me run
    And I will strive with things impossible,   325
    Yea, get the better of them. What's to do?
BRUTUS A piece of work that will make sick men whole.
LIGARIUS But are not some whole that we must make sick?
BRUTUS That must we also. What it is, my Caius,
    I shall unfold to thee as we are going   330
    To whom it must be done.
LIGARIUS   Set on your foot,
    And with a heart new fired I follow you
    To do I know not what; but it sufficeth
    That Brutus leads me on.
                 Thunder
BRUTUS   Follow me then.
                        Exeunt

Caesar tells how his wife Calpurnia has spoken of his murder in her sleep. She orders him to stay at home, telling of frightening portents of ill omen. Caesar is unmoved, declaring he will go out.

1 At home with Brutus and Caesar (in groups of three)

Briefly rehearse 2.1.229–36 and 2.2.1–12. (with or without a director). Act them out to another group.

Discuss everything that you notice is different about the lives of Brutus and Caesar.

2 The cries of dumb animals (in groups of five)

Animals are not silent when slaughtered. While Calpurnia speaks, the priests are making sacrifices for Caesar, who was the chief priest (Pontifex Maximus).

While two or three persons read aloud lines 13–26, dividing it by full stops and semi-colons, the others make the anguished cries of animals being slaughtered not far away. Change roles and repeat the activity.

Would such a staging add something useful to this scene? Does it fit your personal image of Caesar himself and Rome as a whole?

3 Always I am Caesar (in groups of four)

Caesar often refers to himself not as 'I' or 'me', but as 'Caesar'.

Try holding a conversation with your friends where you always refer to yourself by your surname. Topics can range from what you had for breakfast to your grandest personal ambitions.

Afterwards, talk together about the effect it had on your conversation. Then discuss why Caesar does it.

---

watch night patrol (watchmen)
whelpèd given birth
use usual experience

ACT 2 SCENE 2
Caesar's house   Early morning

Thunder and lightning. Enter JULIUS CAESAR *in his nightgown*

CAESAR Nor heaven nor earth have been at peace tonight.
Thrice hath Calpurnia in her sleep cried out,
'Help ho, they murder Caesar!' Who's within?

Enter a SERVANT

SERVANT My lord?
CAESAR Go bid the priests do present sacrifice   5
And bring me their opinions of success.
SERVANT I will, my lord.   *Exit*

Enter CALPURNIA

CALPURNIA What mean you, Caesar, think you to walk forth?
You shall not stir out of your house today.
CAESAR Caesar shall forth. The things that threatened me   10
Ne'er looked but on my back; when they shall see
The face of Caesar they are vanishèd.
CALPURNIA Caesar, I never stood on ceremonies,
Yet now they fright me. There is one within,
Besides the things that we have heard and seen,   15
Recounts most horrid sights seen by the watch.
A lioness hath whelpèd in the streets,
And graves have yawned and yielded up their dead;
Fierce fiery warriors fight upon the clouds
In ranks and squadrons and right form of war,   20
Which drizzled blood upon the Capitol;
The noise of battle hurtled in the air,
Horses did neigh and dying men did groan,
And ghosts did shriek and squeal about the streets.
O Caesar, these things are beyond all use,   25
And I do fear them.
CAESAR   What can be avoided
Whose end is purposed by the mighty gods?
Yet Caesar shall go forth, for these predictions
Are to the world in general as to Caesar.

> *Death holds no fear for Caesar. He defies the auguries, yet they and*
> *Calpurnia prevail. Caesar orders Decius to tell the Senate that*
> *Caesar will not come today.*

1 The Caesar tapes (in pairs or groups of three)

President Nixon of the United States was so suspicious that he bugged and taped every conversation in the White House, including his own. The tapes later became damaging evidence when he faced charges of corruption. Before release to the court, months of conversation were 'cleaned up' by his staff.

After Caesar's death, Antony and Octavius want to present a favourable image of Caesar. Imagine they ask you to edit a tape of this scene from lines 1–56.

a You will quickly see that the same words can be interpreted differently. Find passages which fit both these interpretations of Caesar.

Favourable	*Unfavourable*
Valiant soldier	Bragging coward
God-fearing priest	Superstitious heathen
Shrewd philosopher	Image-conscious politician
Tender husband	Husband besotted with wife

b Find those words or phrases in lines 1–56 that show Caesar to be unworthy. Read or tape record the lines omitting your chosen words. Does your version now show that his decision to stay at home is honourable?

c Compare your edited version with that of another group, explaining your out-takes.

CALPURNIA When beggars die there are no comets seen,   30
     The heavens themselves blaze forth the death of princes.
CAESAR Cowards die many times before their deaths,
     The valiant never taste of death but once.
     Of all the wonders that I yet have heard
     It seems to me most strange that men should fear,   35
     Seeing that death, a necessary end,
     Will come when it will come.

Enter a SERVANT

                   What say the augurers?
SERVANT They would not have you to stir forth today.
     Plucking the entrails of an offering forth,
     They could not find a heart within the beast.   40
CAESAR The gods do this in shame of cowardice.
     Caesar should be a beast without a heart
     If he should stay at home today for fear.
     No, Caesar shall not. Danger knows full well
     That Caesar is more dangerous than he: 45
     We are two lions littered in one day,
     And I the elder and more terrible.
     And Caesar shall go forth.
CALPURNIA   Alas, my lord,
     Your wisdom is consumed in confidence.
     Do not go forth today. Call it my fear   50
     That keeps you in the house, and not your own.
     We'll send Mark Antony to the Senate House
     And he shall say you are not well today.
     Let me, upon my knee, prevail in this.
CAESAR Mark Antony shall say I am not well,   55
     And for thy humour I will stay at home.

Enter DECIUS

     Here's Decius Brutus, he shall tell them so.
DECIUS Caesar, all hail! Good morrow, worthy Caesar,
     I come to fetch you to the Senate House.
CAESAR And you are come in very happy time   60
     To bear my greeting to the senators
     And tell them that I will not come today.
     Cannot is false, and that I dare not, falser:
     I will not come today. Tell them so, Decius.

Calpurnia suggests that Decius should say Caesar is sick. Caesar scorns the lie and describes Calpurnia's dream. Decius interprets it favourably and says the Senate intend to crown Caesar.

1 Calpurnia's dream

Copy this statue of Caesar. Add the spouts of blood and the smiling Romans, referred to in lines 76–89.

2 The dream interpreted in two ways (in pairs)

Both conspirators and Caesarites could make use of Calpurnia's prophetic dream to justify or condemn Caesar's assassination after the event.

Working as professional speech writers, justify or condemn the conspiracy, making this dream the basis of your speech.

3 'Tinctures, stains, relics and cognisance'

Two ideas are brought together in line 89. As a martyr, relics dipped in Caesar's blood ('tinctured' or coloured) are holy. As a prince, he dispenses colours or 'tinctures' that can be put on a coat of arms – recognition or 'cognisance' by a royal personage. Both ideas flatter Caesar and both are repugnant to a true Republican.

In the Roman Catholic church, relics of saints were put in beautiful gold and jewelled boxes called reliquaries. Design a reliquary or a coat of arms which expresses your loyalty to Caesar after his death.

CALPURNIA Say he is sick.

CAESAR   Shall Caesar send a lie?   65
　　　　Have I in conquest stretched mine arm so far
　　　　To be afeard to tell greybeards the truth?
　　　　Decius, go tell them Caesar will not come.

DECIUS Most mighty Caesar, let me know some cause,
　　　　Lest I be laughed at when I tell them so.   70

CAESAR The cause is in my will. I will not come:
　　　　That is enough to satisfy the Senate.
　　　　But for your private satisfaction,
　　　　Because I love you, I will let you know:
　　　　Calpurnia here, my wife, stays me at home.   75
　　　　She dreamt tonight she saw my statue,
　　　　Which like a fountain with an hundred spouts
　　　　Did run pure blood, and many lusty Romans
　　　　Came smiling and did bathe their hands in it.
　　　　And these does she apply for warnings and portents   80
　　　　And evils imminent, and on her knee
　　　　Hath begged that I will stay at home today.

DECIUS This dream is all amiss interpreted,
　　　　It was a vision fair and fortunate.
　　　　Your statue spouting blood in many pipes,   85
　　　　In which so many smiling Romans bathed,
　　　　Signifies that from you great Rome shall suck
　　　　Reviving blood and that great men shall press
　　　　For tinctures, stains, relics, and cognisance.
　　　　This by Calpurnia's dream is signified.   90

CAESAR And this way have you well expounded it.

DECIUS I have, when you have heard what I can say.
　　　　And know it now: the Senate have concluded
　　　　To give this day a crown to mighty Caesar.
　　　　If you shall send them word you will not come,   95
　　　　Their minds may change. Besides, it were a mock
　　　　Apt to be rendered for someone to say,
　　　　'Break up the Senate till another time,
　　　　When Caesar's wife shall meet with better dreams.'

Caesar resolves to go to the Senate. First the conspirators, then Antony arrive. Caesar offers wine while he prepares himself. The conspirators confide their true intentions.

1 Married to the great (in groups of three)

The careers of major politicians can be made or broken by their spouses.

Portia and Calpurnia are very different. Imagine they meet at a cocktail party given by Caesar. They talk about their role as the wives of eminent Romans. Bring Cassius' wife in too. Her character will be entirely your own creation.

2 The heavens above (in pairs)

Dawn is hinted at 2.1.101 before 3.00 a.m., but the storm could make daybreak fitful. Shakespeare often uses effects of light and weather to suggest the mood of a scene. In today's theatre, light and sound are used as special effects to help the words create the mood.

You are in charge of the thunderstorm tape and the lighting board. Both are calibrated on a scale of 0–10. Your task is to plot the sound and light effects to reflect changes in the characters and action as well as the weather and time of day.

Remember that the speed with which sound and lights are brought up or down is as important as how intense they are.

3 Murmurs of conspiracy (in groups of four)

At the end of the scene we hear the secret thoughts of the conspirators.

On the way to the Capitol, you and another conspirator lag behind with Decius. You talk, among other things, about how Caesar was persuaded to come to the Senate.

As you talk, Cassius catches up. You ask why he was absent.

ague fever
earns grieves

If Caesar hide himself, shall they not whisper, 100
'Lo, Caesar is afraid'?
Pardon me, Caesar, for my dear dear love
To your proceeding bids me tell you this,
And reason to my love is liable.

CAESAR How foolish do your fears seem now, Calpurnia! 105
I am ashamèd I did yield to them.
Give me my robe, for I will go.

Enter BRUTUS, *Ligarius, Metellus, Casca,* TREBONIUS, *Cinna, and* PUBLIUS

And look where Publius is come to fetch me.
PUBLIUS Good morrow, Caesar.
CAESAR   Welcome, Publius.
What, Brutus, are you stirred so early too? 110
Good morrow, Casca. Caius Ligarius,
Caesar was ne'er so much your enemy
As that same ague which hath made you lean.
What is't o'clock?
BRUTUS   Caesar, 'tis strucken eight.
CAESAR I thank you for your pains and courtesy. 115

Enter ANTONY

See, Antony, that revels long a-nights,
Is notwithstanding up. Good morrow, Antony.
ANTONY So to most noble Caesar.
CAESAR [*To Calpurnia*]   Bid them prepare within,
                                    [*Exit Calpurnia*]
I am to blame to be thus waited for.
Now, Cinna, now, Metellus. What, Trebonius, 120
I have an hour's talk in store for you.
Remember that you call on me today;
Be near me that I may remember you.
TREBONIUS Caesar, I will. [*Aside*] And so near will I be
That your best friends shall wish I had been further. 125
CAESAR Good friends, go in and taste some wine with me,
And we, like friends, will straightway go together.
BRUTUS [*Aside*] That every like is not the same, O Caesar,
The heart of Brutus earns to think upon.

                                    Exeunt

Artemidorus reads out the warning he intends to give Caesar. Sending
Lucius to the Capitol, Portia confides how she can hardly hide her worries.

---

1 Artemidorus gives evidence

Imagine you are Artemidorus. Take each or some of the conspirators
named in your paper and put together evidence which will substan-
tiate your suspicions about them. You can make up details but keep
close to the spirit of the play. Perhaps you have a 'mole' among the
conspirators and a dossier on each. Remember you have signed the
paper and it may come up in court.

2 Arguing with the director
(in groups A and B of two or three each)

Many directors cut Shakespeare to shorten the playing time. Group A
are directors who want to cut 2.3 and 2.4. Group B are actors in these
scenes who protest. Both groups must make their case clearly.

Perhaps other scenes should go!

3 Three commonplaces (in groups of up to five)

Commonplaces of everyday sayings make good starting points for
improvisations. Here are three you can explore:

'Every like is not the same' (2.2.128)

'Virtue cannot live/Out of the teeth of emulation' (this means
'excellence' is always threatened by those who also want to be
considered 'excellent' 2.3.11)

'How hard it is for women to keep counsel!' (2.4.9).

---

suitor petitioner

ACT 2 SCENE 3
Rome   A street

Enter ARTEMIDORUS [reading a paper]

ARTEMIDORUS 'Caesar, beware of Brutus, take heed of Cassius, come
not near Casca, have an eye to Cinna, trust not Trebonius, mark well
Metellus Cimber, Decius Brutus loves thee not, thou hast wronged
Caius Ligarius. There is but one mind in all these men, and it is bent
against Caesar. If thou beest not immortal look about you: security   5
gives way to conspiracy. The mighty gods defend thee!

                                   Thy lover,
                                   Artemidorus.'

Here will I stand till Caesar pass along,
And as a suitor will I give him this.
My heart laments that virtue cannot live   10
Out of the teeth of emulation.
If thou read this, O Caesar, thou mayst live;
If not, the fates with traitors do contrive.   *Exit*

ACT 2 SCENE 4
Rome   A street

Enter PORTIA and LUCIUS

PORTIA I prithee, boy, run to the Senate House.
      Stay not to answer me but get thee gone.
      Why dost thou stay?
LUCIUS   To know my errand, madam.
PORTIA I would have had thee there and here again
      Ere I can tell thee what thou shouldst do there.   5
      [*Aside*] O constancy, be strong upon my side,
      Set a huge mountain 'tween my heart and tongue!
      I have a man's mind, but a woman's might.
      How hard it is for women to keep counsel! –
      Art thou here yet?
LUCIUS   Madam, what should I do?   10
      Run to the Capitol, and nothing else?
      And so return to you, and nothing else?

Portia sends Lucius to report back to her what Brutus says and does.
The Soothsayer foresees harm to Caesar, but crowds make his
warning difficult to deliver.

1 Listening to the wind (in pairs or groups of three)

Sometimes, listening for an all-important sound – the door, the telephone, a car – we can concentrate on nothing else and seem forgetful and stupid.

- Whisper lines 10–20. Leave a long listening pause at the end of line 16 and start of line 20. One of you can make sound effects.
- All of you are Portia, straining to hear sounds from the Capitol. As you listen, whisper your suspicions, hopes and fears for what this moment means to your life.
- Gather Portia's thoughts into a poem, where every line starts 'Listen. In the wind I hear . . .'.

2 The power of the Soothsayer (in groups of three or more)

Think of a short but dramatic 'human interest' story you remember from the news. Talk together about how it would have been if a soothsayer told the people what was to happen.

Work the resulting story up into an improvisation. Try to make your soothsayer a character we can believe in today and not a stagey weirdo.

Finally act out lines 21–46, thinking hard about why Portia nearly faints when she has talked to the Soothsayer.

---

sooth truth
suit petition
praetors chief justices

PORTIA Yes, bring me word, boy, if thy lord look well,
        For he went sickly forth, and take good note
        What Caesar doth, what suitors press to him.   15
        Hark, boy, what noise is that?
LUCIUS I hear none, madam.
PORTIA   Prithee listen well:
        I heard a bustling rumour, like a fray,
        And the wind brings it from the Capitol.
LUCIUS Sooth, madam, I hear nothing.   20

                Enter the SOOTHSAYER

PORTIA Come hither, fellow, which way hast thou been?
SOOTHSAYER At mine own house, good lady.
PORTIA What is't o'clock?
SOOTHSAYER   About the ninth hour, lady.
PORTIA Is Caesar yet gone to the Capitol?
SOOTHSAYER Madam, not yet. I go to take my stand   25
        To see him pass on to the Capitol.
PORTIA Thou hast some suit to Caesar, hast thou not?
SOOTHSAYER That I have, lady, if it will please Caesar
        To be so good to Caesar as to hear me:
        I shall beseech him to befriend himself.   30
PORTIA Why, know'st thou any harm's intended towards him?
SOOTHSAYER None that I know will be, much that I fear may chance.
        Good morrow to you. Here the street is narrow:
        The throng that follows Caesar at the heels,
        Of senators, of praetors, common suitors,   35
        Will crowd a feeble man almost to death.
        I'll get me to a place more void, and there
        Speak to great Caesar as he comes along.   *Exit*
PORTIA I must go in. [*Aside*] Ay me, how weak a thing
        The heart of woman is! O Brutus,   40
        The heavens speed thee in thine enterprise!
        Sure the boy heard me. Brutus hath a suit
        That Caesar will not grant. O, I grow faint. –
        Run, Lucius, and commend me to my lord,
        Say I am merry. Come to me again   45
        And bring me word what he doth say to thee.
                                    Exeunt [*severally*]

72

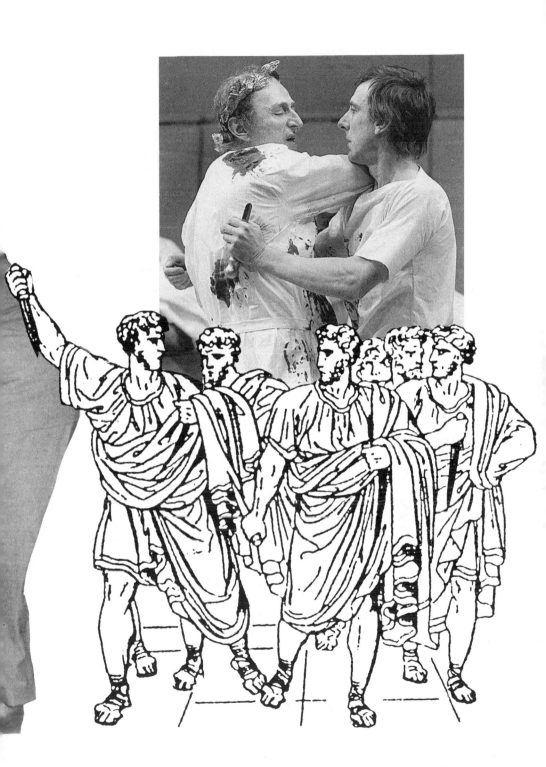

Caesar, in the press of suitors, does not heed attempted warnings. Cassius,
on edge, misinterprets a senator's good wishes. Brutus reassures him.
Trebonius draws Antony away.

---

1 Caesar enters the Capitol

At least fifteen characters enter,
to the sound of a flourish – a
blast of trumpets. Make an
enlarged sketch of this drawing
of the Swan Theatre (1595). On
it, work out where Shakespeare
might have moved each
character, bearing in mind the
change from street to Capitol at
line 12. Show where everyone is
at line 18. (For a description of
Caesar's walk to the Capitol read
2.4.34–36.)

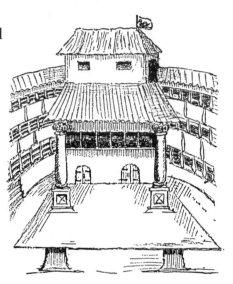

2 Design the set

Design your own set for this scene and show how it works for lines
1–26.

3 With the benefit of hindsight (in pairs)

Experienced politicians can read the progress of friends and enemies
by watching behaviour outside the debating chamber as well as in
session. They notice who talks to whom, reactions, the exchange of
glances.

Read up to line 76 and see if, looking back, there were warning
signs. Talk over the events as if you are senators who were there,
using your imagination to fill in the details: who was where, how they
behaved. Perhaps you heard snatches of conversation which only now
make sense.

ACT 3   SCENE 1
Rome   The Capitol

Flourish. Enter CAESAR, BRUTUS, CASSIUS, CASCA, DECIUS,
METELLUS, TREBONIUS, CINNA, ANTONY, Lepidus, ARTEMIDORUS,
PUBLIUS, POPILLIUS, Ligarius, and the SOOTHSAYER

CAESAR The Ides of March are come.

SOOTHSAYER Ay, Caesar, but not gone.

ARTEMIDORUS Hail, Caesar! Read this schedule.

DECIUS Trebonius doth desire you to o'er-read
          (At your best leisure) this his humble suit.   5

ARTEMIDORUS O Caesar, read mine first, for mine's a suit
          That touches Caesar nearer. Read it, great Caesar.

CAESAR What touches us ourself shall be last served.

ARTEMIDORUS Delay not, Caesar, read it instantly.

CAESAR What, is the fellow mad?

PUBLIUS   Sirrah, give place.   10

CASSIUS What, urge you your petitions in the street?
          Come to the Capitol.
              [*Caesar enters the Capitol, the rest following*]

POPILLIUS I wish your enterprise today may thrive.

CASSIUS What enterprise, Popillius?

POPILLIUS   Fare you well.
              [*Leaves him and joins Caesar*]

BRUTUS What said Popillius Lena?   15

CASSIUS He wished today our enterprise might thrive.
          I fear our purpose is discoverèd.

BRUTUS Look how he makes to Caesar, mark him.

CASSIUS Casca, be sudden, for we fear prevention.
          Brutus, what shall be done? If this be known   20
          Cassius or Caesar never shall turn back,
          For I will slay myself.

BRUTUS   Cassius, be constant.
          Popillius Lena speaks not of our purposes,
          For look he smiles, and Caesar doth not change.

CASSIUS Trebonius knows his time, for look you, Brutus,   25
          He draws Mark Antony out of the way.
              [*Exeunt Antony and Trebonius*]

75

Repeal my brother's banishment, Metellus begs Caesar. Brutus and
Cassius support him and get nearer to Caesar. Caesar adamantly
refuses them all.

1 Publius Cimber is banished (in groups of five or six)

Get Publius Cimber's family to tell one or more of the conspirators
about Publius, his banishment and what Caesar's banishment has
meant to them (the Cimber family can make up the details).

2 Caesar v. the rest (in groups of four)

In quick succession, making Caesar your focus, read Metellus'
speech at line 33, Brutus' at line 52 (with Caesar's response) and
Cassius' at line 55. Do this several times, giving everyone the chance
to be Caesar.

Now look closely at Caesar's two long speeches and talk together
about how well he copes with the three senators' united stand against
Publius' banishment.

Royal Shakespeare Company, 1983.

puissant powerful
turn preordinance and first
 decree/Into the law of children
 change the law of destiny, which
 was laid down at the beginning of
 time, into a law which children
 might think up

enfranchisement the rights of a
 free Roman citizen
firmament sky

DECIUS Where is Metellus Cimber? Let him go
       And presently prefer his suit to Caesar.
BRUTUS He is addressed, press near and second him.
CINNA Casca, you are the first that rears your hand.   30
CAESAR Are we all ready? What is now amiss
       That Caesar and his Senate must redress?
METELLUS Most high, most mighty, and most puissant Caesar,
       Metellus Cimber throws before thy seat
       An humble heart.
CAESAR   I must prevent thee, Cimber.   35
       These couchings and these lowly courtesies
       Might fire the blood of ordinary men
       And turn preordinance and first decree
       Into the law of children. Be not fond
       To think that Caesar bears such rebel blood   40
       That will be thawed from the true quality
       With that which melteth fools – I mean sweet words,
       Low-crookèd curtsies, and base spaniel fawning.
       Thy brother by decree is banishèd:
       If thou dost bend, and pray, and fawn for him,
       I spurn thee like a cur out of my way.   45
       Know Caesar doth not wrong, nor without cause
       Will he be satisfied.
METELLUS Is there no voice more worthy than my own
       To sound more sweetly in great Caesar's ear   50
       For the repealing of my banished brother?
BRUTUS I kiss thy hand, but not in flattery, Caesar,
       Desiring thee that Publius Cimber may
       Have an immediate freedom of repeal.
CAESAR What, Brutus?
CASSIUS   Pardon, Caesar! Caesar, pardon!   55
       As low as to thy foot doth Cassius fall
       To beg enfranchisement for Publius Cimber.
CAESAR I could be well moved, if I were as you;
       If I could pray to move, prayers would move me.
       But I am constant as the northern star,
       Of whose true-fixed and resting quality   60
       There is no fellow in the firmament.

Having declared himself the world's only constant man, Caesar is stabbed to death. Brutus tries to reassure all who flee, but the conspirators are left alone in the Senate.

1 The assassination (in groups of seven)

Brutus said, 'Let's be sacrificers, but not butchers' (2.1.166), but the conspirators probably kill Caesar in different ways. Each person chooses which conspirator to play. Think about which part of Caesar's body he might choose to stab, and the style in which he would stab.

Carefully stage the assassination. Then, without words, present it to the class either in slow motion or as a still 'snapshot'.

2 Caesar's last speech (in groups of five or more)

Your group is the panel of a current affairs programme discussing Caesar's last speech (lines 58–73). Half are for Caesar, half against him.

Consider the speech in short sections. Your chairperson should pick out points of interest and ask questions. The programme runs for ten to fifteen minutes and your comments sum up everything you think about Caesar.

3 Countdown to assassination (in groups of four)

By changing names and a few words, change lines 33–73 into your class, begging your teacher not to give you a test today. One or two groups could act it out with background noise from the whole class.

This could be comic, but consider the actual request, the conspirators' intentions and the presence of the Senate. How well or badly do the central characters come out of it?

---

apprehensive quick to understand, fearful
Olympus a Greek mountain, home of the gods
bootless without effect
Et tu, Brute? Even you, Brutus?
common pulpits see **Pulpits**, page 174

The skies are painted with unnumbered sparks,
They are all fire, and every one doth shine;
But there's but one in all doth hold his place.   65
So in the world: 'tis furnished well with men,
And men are flesh and blood, and apprehensive;
Yet in the number I do know but one
That unassailable holds on his rank,
Unshaked of motion, and that I am he   70
Let me a little show it, even in this:
That I was constant Cimber should be banished,
And constant do remain to keep him so.

CINNA O Caesar –

CAESAR   Hence! Wilt thou lift up Olympus?

DECIUS Great Caesar –

CAESAR   Doth not Brutus bootless kneel?   75

CASCA Speak hands for me!

                    They stab Caesar

CAESAR *Et tu, Brute?* – Then fall, Caesar!   *Dies*

CINNA Liberty! Freedom! Tyranny is dead!
        Run hence, proclaim, cry it about the streets.

CASSIUS Some to the common pulpits, and cry out,   80
        'Liberty, freedom, and enfranchisement!'

BRUTUS People and senators, be not affrighted,
        Fly not, stand still! Ambition's debt is paid.

CASCA Go to the pulpit, Brutus.

DECIUS   And Cassius too.

BRUTUS Where's Publius?   85

CINNA Here, quite confounded with this mutiny.

METELLUS Stand fast together lest some friend of Caesar's
        Should chance –

BRUTUS Talk not of standing. Publius, good cheer,
        There is no harm intended to your person,   90
        Nor to no Roman else. So tell them, Publius.

CASSIUS And leave us, Publius, lest that the people,
        Rushing on us, should do your age some mischief.

BRUTUS Do so, and let no man abide this deed
        But we the doers.   95

                    [*Exeunt all but the conspirators*]

Julius Caesar

> *Trebonius reports panic outside. The conspirators depart to proclaim*
> *themselves liberators, their daggers and forearms ritually bloodied. They*
> *halt as Antony's servant enters bringing his master's message.*

1 'Peace, freedom and liberty!' (in groups of three to five)

Turn to the pictures on page 73. The line drawings show the
conspirators coming into the market-place after the assassination, but
the artist has left out the blood with which they covered their
forearms and swords in lines 105–18. Talk together about how
different the picture would look if the blood were shown.

Each group is a public relations firm competing to produce the best
corporate image for the Republican cause.

a Assess the advantages and disadvantages of the image Brutus has
   given you (lines 105–10). How well does it express 'Peace, freedom
   and liberty'? Write a short report for Brutus.

b Devise a public relations campaign to persuade Rome that
   Republicanism, not dictatorship or monarchy, is the only way. You
   could:
   - invent a symbol, having assessed the effectiveness of those
     symbols you know (e.g. cross, hammer and sickle, skull and
     crossbones):
   - script a party political broadcast (and perhaps perform or video
     it)
   - write a song (e.g. 'Land of Hope and Glory', 'The Red Flag', or
     'Beasts of England' in *Animal Farm*)
   - design an Ides of March monument or plaque for the Capitol
   - have ideas of your own!

---

doomsday Day of Judgement
stand upon argue about

on Pompey's basis at the foot of
Pompey's statue

Enter TREBONIUS

CASSIUS Where is Antony?

TREBONIUS   Fled to his house amazed.
    Men, wives, and children stare, cry out, and run
    As it were doomsday.

BRUTUS   Fates, we will know your pleasures.
    That we shall die we know: 'tis but the time,
    And drawing days out, that men stand upon.   100

CASCA Why, he that cuts off twenty years of life
    Cuts off so many years of fearing death.

BRUTUS Grant that, and then is death a benefit.
    So are we Caesar's friends, that have abridged
    His time of fearing death. Stoop, Romans, stoop,   105
    And let us bathe our hands in Caesar's blood
    Up to the elbows and besmear our swords.
    Then walk we forth, even to the market-place,
    And waving our red weapons o'er our heads
    Let's all cry, 'Peace, freedom, and liberty!'   110

CASSIUS Stoop then and wash. How many ages hence
    Shall this our lofty scene be acted over
    In states unborn and accents yet unknown!

BRUTUS How many times shall Caesar bleed in sport,
    That now on Pompey's basis lies along   115
    No worthier than the dust!

CASSIUS   So oft as that shall be,
    So often shall the knot of us be called
    The men that gave their country liberty.

DECIUS What, shall we forth?

CASSIUS   Ay, every man away.
    Brutus shall lead, and we will grace his heels   120
    With the most boldest and best hearts of Rome.

Enter a SERVANT

BRUTUS Soft, who comes here? A friend of Antony's.

SERVANT Thus, Brutus, did my master bid me kneel,
    Thus did Mark Antony bid me fall down,
    And, being prostrate, thus he bade me say: 125
    Brutus is noble, wise, valiant, and honest;
    Caesar was mighty, bold, royal, and loving.

Antony's servant says that if Brutus' reasons for murder are convincing, Antony will follow Brutus. Brutus grants safe access to Antony who enters and offers to be killed with Caesar.

---

1 Mark Antony – trustworthy or treacherous? (in pairs)

Cassius says before Mark Antony's entry 'my misgiving still/Falls shrewdly to the purpose'. His suspicions turn out to be right. Hold a secret conversation with a fellow conspirator, in which you try to find reasons for Cassius' continuing suspicion. Analyse the servant's speech closely for deliberately vague or misleading phrases, especially about Brutus and Caesar.

2 Home gangs and Rome gangs
(in groups A and B of four or five each)

Two big gangs A and B, always at war, run your area. Give them vivid names. You belong to one.

In gang A the leader has just been sent to prison, given away by a member of gang B. Nobody in gang A has the power to replace him. His best friend comes to gang B with a proposal. Could gang A join gang B?

In a session with your own gang, fill in the details then work out how to approach or receive your enemy. Can either of you trust each other after the years of battle and bad feeling?

Then improvise the meeting.

After the meeting, hold a session with your own gang to assess how it went and what the next move is. Compare your situation to that in 3.1, opposite.

---

presently at once
rank rotten or diseased

purpled Antony says Caesar's blood is the colour of royalty

Say I love Brutus, and I honour him;
Say I feared Caesar, honoured him, and loved him.
If Brutus will vouchsafe that Antony   130
May safely come to him and be resolved
How Caesar hath deserved to lie in death,
Mark Antony shall not love Caesar dead
So well as Brutus living, but will follow
The fortunes and affairs of noble Brutus   135
Through the hazards of this untrod state
With all true faith. So says my master Antony.

BRUTUS Thy master is a wise and valiant Roman,
I never thought him worse.
Tell him, so please him come unto this place,   140
He shall be satisfied and by my honour
Depart untouched.

SERVANT   I'll fetch him presently.   *Exit Servant*

BRUTUS I know that we shall have him well to friend.

CASSIUS I wish we may. But yet have I a mind
That fears him much, and my misgiving still   145
Falls shrewdly to the purpose.

Enter ANTONY

BRUTUS But here comes Antony. Welcome, Mark Antony!

ANTONY O mighty Caesar! Dost thou lie so low?
Are all thy conquests, glories, triumphs, spoils
Shrunk to this little measure? Fare thee well!   150
I know not, gentlemen, what you intend,
Who else must be let blood, who else is rank.
If I myself, there is no hour so fit
As Caesar's death's hour, nor no instrument
Of half that worth as those your swords made rich   155
With the most noble blood of all this world.
I do beseech ye, if you bear me hard,
Now, whilst your purpled hands do reek and smoke,
Fulfil your pleasure. Live a thousand years,
I shall not find myself so apt to die: 160
No place will please me so, no mean of death,
As here by Caesar, and by you cut off,
The choice and master spirits of this age.

Brutus claims that pity for Rome killed Caesar. Brutus loves Antony and loved Caesar. Antony shakes the conspirators' hands but fears this act of friendship wrongs Caesar.

1 Outward action, secret thoughts (in eight pairs)

At the end of 3.1 we have no doubt about Antony's intentions towards the conspirators, however he behaves towards them here.

Work up a presentation of lines 184–9 in which each character is played by two people. One speaks and behaves as in the scripted action (the *action* player), the other utters secret unscripted thoughts (the *thought* player). When the *thought* player stamps a foot, the action freezes while thoughts are spoken, and resumes with another stamp. *Thought* players shadow *action* players during presentation. Each bloody handshake is cue for a second thought from Antony or a conspirator – or both!

Before presentation, *action* and *thought* players research the script together to find what their character may think of Antony, or he of them. During presentation, *thought* players can improvise or read from notes, but always with appropriate expression and tone of voice – which may be quite different from those of the *action* player!

2 Conspirators – the facts (in groups of three to five)

Apart from Brutus and Cassius, we will not see the six conspirators again. You and your team of reporters have to profile the involvement of each one in the assassination. Give news-hungry Rome a quick character sketch (perhaps with pictures) of the men behind the words and the daggers.

When you have established the main facts, you can make up further details about them and their lives.

---

our arms in strength of malice nobody has a clear interpretation of this line. Any ideas?

dignities positions of influence
conceit think of

BRUTUS O Antony, beg not your death of us.
    Though now we must appear bloody and cruel,   165
    As by our hands and this our present act
    You see we do, yet see you but our hands
    And this the bleeding business they have done.
    Our hearts you see not, they are pitiful;
    And pity to the general wrong of Rome –   170
    As fire drives out fire, so pity pity –
    Hath done this deed on Caesar. For your part,
    To you our swords have leaden points, Mark Antony;
    Our arms in strength of malice, and our hearts
    Of brothers' temper, do receive you in   175
    With all kind love, good thoughts, and reverence.
CASSIUS Your voice shall be as strong as any man's
    In the disposing of new dignities.
BRUTUS Only be patient till we have appeased
    The multitude, beside themselves with fear,   180
    And then we will deliver you the cause
    Why I, that did love Caesar when I struck him,
    Have thus proceeded.
ANTONY   I doubt not of your wisdom.
    Let each man render me his bloody hand.
    First, Marcus Brutus, will I shake with you;   185
    Next, Caius Cassius, do I take your hand;
    Now, Decius Brutus, yours; now yours, Metellus;
    Yours, Cinna; and, my valiant Casca, yours;
    Though last, not least in love, yours, good Trebonius.
    Gentlemen all – alas, what shall I say?   190
    My credit now stands on such slippery ground
    That one of two bad ways you must conceit me,
    Either a coward or a flatterer.
    That I did love thee, Caesar, O, 'tis true.
    If then thy spirit look upon us now,   195
    Shall it not grieve thee dearer than thy death
    To see thy Antony making his peace,
    Shaking the bloody fingers of thy foes –
    Most noble – in the presence of thy corse?
    Had I as many eyes as thou hast wounds,   200
    Weeping as fast as they stream forth thy blood,
    It would become me better than to close
    In terms of friendship with thine enemies.

Julius Caesar

Antony praises Caesar. Cassius asks if Antony intends to show friendship to the conspirators. Yes, replies Antony, if reasons for Caesar's death are given. Cassius is uneasy about Antony speaking at Caesar's funeral.

1 A school for courtiers

Antony brings the world of the royalist and the courtier on stage, sharply contrasting with the blunt Republicans. Reverence, a feeling for beauty and learning, delight in poetic words and ideas were essential to a career at the court of Elizabeth I. The correct thing was to behave towards Elizabeth as if you were a lover without hope and she far above you.

a Compliments (in two groups of five or six each)
An important position must be filled at court. The courtier who makes the most thoughtful, original and beautiful compliment will win it. The approach to the throne is also important. Movement is dignified and respectful.

While the one group plays the monarch and advisers, the other plays the courtiers. Then swap over.

b Moles (in groups of three or four)
You are Republican spies who want to infiltrate 'monarchist' circles. Model your opinions, language, conversation and movement on Antony, and give each other lessons.

And try the reverse process: monarchists passing for Republicans!

2 Brutus gives Antony satisfaction (in groups of three)

Brutus never does explain his actions to Antony, and Antony has promised nothing. But hold the conversation them might have had, joined by Octavius and Cassius.

---

bayed trapped
thy spoil the spilt blood of your flesh
hart deer

Lethe the underworld river which the dead must drink from to forget their mortal lives
pricked marked down

Pardon me, Julius! Here wast thou bayed, brave hart,
Here didst thou fall, and here thy hunters stand, 205
Signed in thy spoil and crimsoned in thy Lethe.
O world! Thou wast the forest to this hart,
And this indeed, O world, the heart of thee.
How like a deer strucken by many princes
Dost thou here lie! 210

CASSIUS Mark Antony –
ANTONY   Pardon me, Caius Cassius,
The enemies of Caesar shall say this;
Then, in a friend, it is cold modesty.

CASSIUS I blame you not for praising Caesar so,
But what compact mean you to have with us? 215
Will you be pricked in number of our friends,
Or shall we on and not depend on you?

ANTONY Therefore I took your hands, but was indeed
Swayed from the point by looking down on Caesar.
Friends am I with you all, and love you all, 220
Upon this hope, that you shall give me reasons
Why and wherein Caesar was dangerous.

BRUTUS Or else were this a savage spectacle.
Our reasons are so full of good regard
That were you, Antony, the son of Caesar 225
You should be satisfied.

ANTONY   That's all I seek,
And am, moreover, suitor that I may
Produce his body to the market-place,
And in the pulpit, as becomes a friend,
Speak in the order of his funeral. 230

BRUTUS You shall, Mark Antony.

CASSIUS   Brutus, a word with you.
[Aside to Brutus] You know not what you do. Do not consent
That Antony speak in his funeral.
Know you how much the people may be moved
By that which he will utter?

BRUTUS [Aside to Cassius]   By your pardon, 235
I will myself into the pulpit first
And show the reason of our Caesar's death.

*Antony is given permission to speak at Caesar's funeral after Brutus,
but not to blame the conspirators. Left alone with Caesar's body,
Antony prophesies horrific civil war.*

It is worth exploring the dramatic impact of this crucial soliloquy
(lines 254–75) from Antony at the halfway point of the play. You can
work on all or some of the speech.

1 A bedtime story (in pairs)

a Read the speech to your partner as a mother would read a pretty
bedtime story to a child whose eyes are shut ready for sleep.

b Get together with one or two other pairs. 'Children' now ask
'mothers' endless questions about what it means ('Mummy, what
does . . . mean?'). 'Mothers' explain in great detail, still in soothing
'bedtime' voices.

c 'Mothers' now shut their eyes while 'children' whisper the speech
into their ears with urgency and menace.

2 Nightmare voices (in groups of five or more)

Work out how you can present this speech with maximum horror.
Use all your voices, sometimes speaking together, sometimes separately or individually. You can repeat or echo words, emphasise sound
patterns and rhythms, build to a crescendo, fade to nothing, be
suddenly loud, suddenly soft. No need to stick to words; you can
make rhythmic, threatening noises or other sounds which the words
suggest. By putting people in different parts of the room you can get
quadrophonic sound.

You may find you know the speech by heart after all this work!

---

cumber trouble or load down
fell savage

Ate the fanatical goddess of
revenge and mischief, banished by
the gods to live among men
carrion men men who are nearly
corpses

88

What Antony shall speak, I will protest
He speaks by leave and by permission,
And that we are contented Caesar shall   240
Have all true rites and lawful ceremonies.
It shall advantage more than do us wrong.
CASSIUS [*Aside to Brutus*] I know not what may fall, I like it not.
BRUTUS Mark Antony, here take you Caesar's body.
You shall not in your funeral speech blame us,   245
But speak all good you can devise of Caesar
And say you do't by our permission,
Else shall you not have any hand at all
About his funeral. And you shall speak
In the same pulpit whereto I am going,   250
After my speech is ended.
ANTONY   Be it so,
I do desire no more.
BRUTUS Prepare the body then and follow us.

Exeunt [all but] Antony

ANTONY O, pardon me, thou bleeding piece of earth,
That I am meek and gentle with these butchers!   255
Thou art the ruins of the noblest man
That ever livèd in the tide of times.
Woe to the hand that shed this costly blood!
Over thy wounds now do I prophesy –
Which like dumb mouths do ope their ruby lips   260
To beg the voice and utterance of my tongue –
A curse shall light upon the limbs of men:
Domestic fury and fierce civil strife
Shall cumber all the parts of Italy;
Blood and destruction shall be so in use   265
And dreadful objects so familiar
That mothers shall but smile when they behold
Their infants quartered with the hands of war,
All pity choked with custom of fell deeds;
And Caesar's spirit, ranging for revenge,   270
With Ate by his side come hot from hell,
Shall in these confines with a monarch's voice
Cry havoc and let slip the dogs of war,
That this foul deed shall smell above the earth
With carrion men groaning for burial.   275

> *Octavius' servant reports his master's approach. Antony suggests that Octavius waits until the people's mood has been tested. In the marketplace, Brutus and Cassius prepare to speak.*

1 The day that Caesar was killed (in groups of three to six)

- Many adults remember the exact time and place they heard of President Kennedy's assassination in 1963. See if you can recreate the moment when a group of ordinary Romans hear of Caesar's death. What questions will they ask?
- Antony says 'Here is a mourning Rome, a dangerous Rome . . .'. Write a report for Octavius about the mood of the city after the assassination.

2 Great speeches in the mouth and in the ear
(in groups of four to six)

The greatest formal oratory Shakespeare wrote is in 3.2. The speeches of Brutus and Mark Antony (lines 13–39 and lines 65–242) have to be read aloud *and listened to* in their entirety for their art to be fully appreciated.

Two or three of you read the speeches aloud, taking a sentence each in turn while the rest listen closely *without following the script*. Leave out the Plebeians' lines. Then swap over. After each speech, talk together about how it felt when you spoke it and how it felt when you listened to it.

3 Cassius' speech to the people

At line 10, Cassius leaves to speak to half the crowd in another street.

Remind yourself of his speeches in 1.2 and 3 and write the speech he might have delivered. The Elizabethan schoolboy's guide to the structure of a speech on page 92 will help you.

Your class could be the crowd to whom you deliver the speech. Remember that they have received news of Caesar's death only moments ago, and are likely to question you.

Octavius Caesar a distant relation of the dictator; his ability recommended itself to Julius who treated him as a son and heir

seven leagues about twenty-one miles

Plebeians ordinary people, workers

Enter Octavio's SERVANT

     You serve Octavius Caesar, do you not?
SERVANT I do, Mark Antony.
ANTONY Caesar did write for him to come to Rome.
SERVANT He did receive his letters, and is coming,
     And bid me say to you by word of mouth –   280
                [*Seeing the body*]
     O Caesar!
ANTONY Thy heart is big, get thee apart and weep.
     Passion, I see, is catching, for mine eyes,
     Seeing those beads of sorrow stand in thine,
     Began to water. Is thy master coming?   285
SERVANT He lies tonight within seven leagues of Rome.
ANTONY Post back with speed and tell him what hath chanced.
     Here is a mourning Rome, a dangerous Rome,
     No Rome of safety for Octavius yet:
     Hie hence and tell him so. Yet stay awhile,   290
     Thou shalt not back till I have borne this corse
     Into the market-place. There shall I try
     In my oration how the people take
     The cruel issue of these bloody men,
     According to the which thou shalt discourse   295
     To young Octavius of the state of things.
     Lend me your hand.
                Exeunt [*with Caesar's body*]

ACT 3   SCENE 2
Rome   The market-place

Enter BRUTUS *and Cassius with the* PLEBEIANS

ALL We will be satisfied! Let us be satisfied!
BRUTUS Then follow me and give me audience, friends.
     Cassius, go you into the other street
     And part the numbers.
     Those that will hear me speak, let 'em stay here;   5

Brutus addresses the people of Rome. He says he loved Rome's freedom more than Caesar, and the crowd accepts it. Antony enters with Caesar's corpse.

1 An Elizabethan lesson in rhetoric (in groups of three)

An Elizabethan schoolboy studied speeches and debating as part of his 'rhetoric' lessons. A classic 'theme' was divided like this in a textbook of the time:

exordium (introduction) to gain the approval of the hearers and their attention
narratio (development) that the listeners may fully understand the matter being discussed
confirmatio (evidence) proofs, arguments and reason, illustrated by quotations
confutatio (dealing with objections) to consider what may be objected against it, and how to answer them
conclusio (summing up) a short recapitulation.

Find the divisions in lines 13–39 of Brutus' speech (where they are very clear) and then in lines 65–242 of Antony's (where they may be less clear).

Try reading one of Brutus' divisions then the same one in Antony's speech, and note the contrast in technique as well as thought and behaviour.

2 Caesar's death enrolled in the Capitol (in pairs)

Brutus says (line 32) that an agreed statement, setting out reasons for Caesar's death, has been officially lodged or 'enrolled' in the Capitol. See if you, as conspirators, can write that document.

3 Enter Mark Antony with Caesar's body

Antony likes plays and, in 3.1, acts well himself!

Put yourself in his place and plan the big entry with Caesar's corpse. Think very carefully about: your own appearance (blood?); how you relate to the corpse; the corpse itself and its presentation ('coffin' at line 98?); and finally where to enter and where to stand while Brutus speaks. You could write notes for yourself to guide your actions.

Those that will follow Cassius, go with him;
And public reasons shall be renderèd
Of Caesar's death.

1 PLEBEIAN   I will hear Brutus speak.

2 PLEBEIAN I will hear Cassius and compare their reasons
When severally we hear them renderèd.   10

> [*Exit Cassius with some of the Plebeians*]
> [*Brutus goes into the pulpit*]

3 PLEBEIAN The noble Brutus is ascended, silence!

BRUTUS Be patient till the last.

Romans, countrymen, and lovers, hear me for my cause, and be silent that you may hear. Believe me for mine honour, and have respect to mine honour that you may believe. Censure me in your wisdom, and   15
awake your senses that you may the better judge. If there be any in this assembly, any dear friend of Caesar's, to him I say that Brutus' love to Caesar was no less than his. If then that friend demand why Brutus rose against Caesar, this is my answer: not that I loved Caesar less, but that I loved Rome more. Had you rather Caesar were living, and   20
die all slaves, than that Caesar were dead, to live all freemen? As Caesar loved me, I weep for him; as he was fortunate, I rejoice at it; as he was valiant, I honour him; but, as he was ambitious, I slew him. There is tears for his love, joy for his fortune, honour for his valour, and death for his ambition. Who is here so base that would be a   25
bondman? If any, speak, for him have I offended. Who is here so rude that would not be a Roman? If any, speak, for him have I offended. Who is here so vile that will not love his country? If any, speak, for him have I offended. I pause for a reply.

ALL None, Brutus, none.   30

BRUTUS Then none have I offended. I have done no more to Caesar than you shall do to Brutus. The question of his death is enrolled in the Capitol, his glory not extenuated wherein he was worthy, nor his offences enforced for which he suffered death.

Enter MARK ANTONY [*and others*] *with Caesar's body*

Here comes his body, mourned by Mark Antony, who, though he had   35
no hand in his death, shall receive the benefit of his dying, a place in the commonwealth, as which of you shall not? With this I depart: that, as I slew my best lover for the good of Rome, I have the same dagger for myself when it shall please my country to need my death.

> [*Comes down*]

Julius Caesar

Hailed as a new leader, Brutus asks the crowd to hear Antony out. In the pulpit, Antony at first seems to reflect the anti-Caesar mood of the crowd.

1 The morning papers get it wrong (in pairs)

- Imagine that the notes of the reporter for *The Argus* got muddled up, so Brutus started 'Friends, Romans, countrymen' and Antony 'Romans, countrymen and lovers'. Write a letter to *The Argus* which shows how the choice and order of the words foreshadow the content and emphasis of the speeches, and that their coverage must, therefore, be wrong.

- Notes about Cassius' speech were lost completely. Guess at his opening line, using your knowledge of the man and his beliefs. Compare your guesses with those of other groups.

2 The speaker's craft (in groups of three to four)

Good speakers learn by listening to experienced orators.

- Between lines 65 and 151 of Antony's speech you will find five or six key words (such as ambition/ambitious) emphasised and repeated seven to fifteen times each. Find some of them and work out what effect the repetition has.

- Imagine you are a group of young senators comparing the techniques of persuasion used by your seniors, not only with a plebeian crowd (as here and in 1.1), but also in the Senate or on a one-to-one basis. You could review the words of different speakers in different situations in the play, choosing and reviewing examples of poorer quality work. Sum up your findings in a list of useful tips for speakers.

beholding to obliged to
interrèd buried

ALL Live, Brutus, live, live!   40

1 PLEBEIAN Bring him with triumph home unto his house.

2 PLEBEIAN Give him a statue with his ancestors.

3 PLEBEIAN Let him be Caesar.

4 PLEBEIAN   Caesar's better parts
     Shall be crowned in Brutus.

1 PLEBEIAN   We'll bring him to his house
     With shouts and clamours.

BRUTUS   My countrymen –   45

2 PLEBEIAN Peace, silence, Brutus speaks!

1 PLEBEIAN   Peace ho!

BRUTUS Good countrymen, let me depart alone,
     And, for my sake, stay here with Antony.
     Do grace to Caesar's corpse, and grace his speech
     Tending to Caesar's glories, which Mark Antony   50
     (By our permission) is allowed to make.
     I do entreat you, not a man depart,
     Save I alone, till Antony have spoke.   *Exit*

1 PLEBEIAN Stay ho, and let us hear Mark Antony.

3 PLEBEIAN Let him go up into the public chair,   55
     We'll hear him. Noble Antony, go up.

ANTONY For Brutus' sake, I am beholding to you.
             [Goes into the pulpit]

4 PLEBEIAN What does he say of Brutus?

3 PLEBEIAN   He says for Brutus' sake
     He finds himself beholding to us all.

4 PLEBEIAN 'Twere best he speak no harm of Brutus here!   60

1 PLEBEIAN This Caesar was a tyrant.

3 PLEBEIAN   Nay, that's certain:
     We are blest that Rome is rid of him.

2 PLEBEIAN Peace, let us hear what Antony can say.

ANTONY You gentle Romans –

ALL   Peace ho, let us hear him.

ANTONY Friends, Romans, countrymen, lend me your ears!   65
     I come to bury Caesar, not to praise him.
     The evil that men do lives after them,
     The good is oft interrèd with their bones:
     So let it be with Caesar. The noble Brutus
     Hath told you Caesar was ambitious;   70
     If it were so, it was a grievous fault,
     And grievously hath Caesar answered it.

While appearing to agree with Brutus' portrait of Caesar, Antony rejects it in reality by listing Caesar's virtues. The crowd becomes uncertain, swayed by Antony's grief.

1 My Dad, the First Plebeian (in groups of five or six)

You were with your father, the First Plebeian, and heard him shout these things:

'This Caesar was a tyrant' (line 61)
'Methinks there is much reason in his sayings' (line 100)
'Stand from the hearse, stand from the body' (line 156)
'O piteous spectacle! . . . O most bloody sight!' (lines 189 and 193)
'We'll burn the house of Brutus' (line 221).

After the speech you go home, but your father stays out (see 3.3). Tell your mother about your father's remarks and explain what Antony had said before each one so she understands the context. You could explain one remark each.

2 What happened at the Lupercal? (in groups of four)

In 1.2.220–67 Casca tells a more complicated story of what happened at the Lupercal than Antony does in lines 87–9. So does Plutarch on pages 178–80.

While two of you challenge Antony's version, two of you defend Antony's point of view that Caesar's behaviour showed no ambition.

---

general coffers chests of money
  for the public good
abide pay for

Here, under leave of Brutus and the rest –
For Brutus is an honourable man,
So are they all, all honourable men –   75
Come I to speak in Caesar's funeral.
He was my friend, faithful and just to me,
But Brutus says he was ambitious,
And Brutus is an honourable man.
He hath brought many captives home to Rome,   80
Whose ransoms did the general coffers fill;
Did this in Caesar seem ambitious?
When that the poor have cried, Caesar hath wept:
Ambition should be made of sterner stuff;
Yet Brutus says he was ambitious,   85
And Brutus is an honourable man.
You all did see that on the Lupercal
I thrice presented him a kingly crown,
Which he did thrice refuse. Was this ambition?
Yet Brutus says he was ambitious,   90
And sure he is an honourable man.
I speak not to disprove what Brutus spoke,
But here I am to speak what I do know.
You all did love him once, not without cause;
What cause withholds you then to mourn for him?   95
O judgement, thou art fled to brutish beasts,
And men have lost their reason! Bear with me,
My heart is in the coffin there with Caesar,
And I must pause till it come back to me.

1 PLEBEIAN Methinks there is much reason in his sayings.   100
2 PLEBEIAN If thou consider rightly of the matter,
Caesar has had great wrong.
3 PLEBEIAN   Has he, masters!
I fear there will a worse come in his place.
4 PLEBEIAN Marked ye his words? He would not take the crown,
Therefore 'tis certain he was not ambitious.   105
1 PLEBEIAN If it be found so, some will dear abide it.
2 PLEBEIAN Poor soul, his eyes are red as fire with weeping.
3 PLEBEIAN There's not a nobler man in Rome than Antony.
4 PLEBEIAN Now mark him, he begins again to speak.

Antony pleads that the plebeians must *remain loyal to the conspirators, and that he* must *wrong Caesar by refusing to let them know how generous his will is to them. Read it! they shout.*

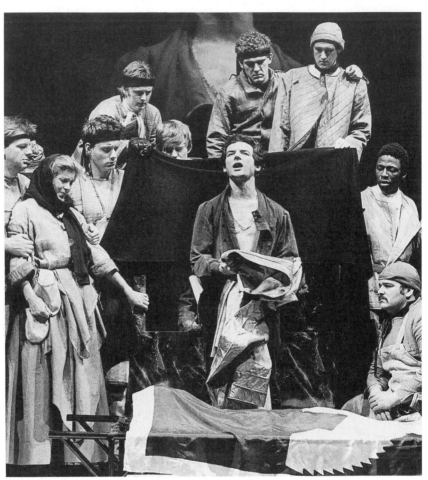

Royal Shakespeare Company, 1983.

closet private room
commons ordinary people

napkins handkerchiefs
issue children

ANTONY   But yesterday the word of Caesar might   110
         Have stood against the world; now lies he there,
         And none so poor to do him reverence.
         O masters, if I were disposed to stir
         Your hearts and minds to mutiny and rage,
         I should do Brutus wrong and Cassius wrong,   115
         Who (you all know) are honourable men.
         I will not do them wrong; I rather choose
         To wrong the dead, to wrong myself and you,
         Than I will wrong such honourable men.
         But here's a parchment with the seal of Caesar,   120
         I found it in his closet, 'tis his will.
         Let but the commons hear this testament –
         Which, pardon me, I do not mean to read –
         And they would go and kiss dead Caesar's wounds
         And dip their napkins in his sacred blood,   125
         Yea, beg a hair of him for memory,
         And, dying, mention it within their wills,
         Bequeathing it as a rich legacy
         Unto their issue.
4 PLEBEIAN   We'll hear the will. Read it, Mark Antony.   130
ALL   The will, the will, we will hear Caesar's will!
ANTONY   Have patience, gentle friends, I must not read it.
         It is not meet you know how Caesar loved you:
         You are not wood, you are not stones, but men,
         And, being men, hearing the will of Caesar,   135
         It will inflame you, it will make you mad.
         'Tis good you know not that you are his heirs,
         For if you should, O, what would come of it?
4 PLEBEIAN   Read the will, we'll hear it, Antony.
         You shall read us the will, Caesar's will!   140
ANTONY   Will you be patient? Will you stay awhile?
         I have o'ershot myself to tell you of it.
         I fear I wrong the honourable men
         Whose daggers have stabbed Caesar, I do fear it.
4 PLEBEIAN   They were traitors. Honourable men!   145
ALL   The will! The testament!
2 PLEBEIAN   They were villains, murderers! The will, read the will!
ANTONY   You will compel me then to read the will?

99

Julius Caesar

*Obeying the crowd, Antony comes down to show them Caesar's corpse,
starting with the dagger cuts in his cloak. The plebeians weep.*

---

1 'Passion, I see, is catching' (in groups of three or four)
Here is part of a police report about a murder by Jack the Ripper:

> I beg to report . . . the murder of Elizabeth Stride on the morning of 30
> September 1888.
>
> 1 a.m. 30 September. A body of a woman was found with the throat cut,
> but not otherwise mutilated, by Louis Diemschutz . . . inside the gates of
> Dutfield's Yard in Berner Street, . . . who gave information to the police.
> P.C. 252 Lamb proceeded with him to the spot and sent for Drs Blackwell
> and Phillips.
>
> 1.10 a.m. Body examined by the doctors mentioned who pronounced life
> extinct; the position of the body was as follows: lying on the left side, left
> arm extended from elbow, cachous lying in hand, right arm over stomach,
> back of hand and inner surface of wrist dotted with blood, legs drawn up,
> knees fixed, feet close to the wall, body still warm, silk handkerchief round
> throat slightly torn corresponding to the angle of right jaw, throat deeply
> gashed and below the right angle apparent abrasion of skin about an inch
> and a quarter in diameter.
>
> Search was made in the yard but no instrument found.

Even though this was Jack the Ripper's third or possibly sixth murder,
the language is precise and unemotional.

Read 3.1 closely, and write a police report about Caesar's murder.
Compare it with Mark Antony's account in lines 160–96. Just as a
jury has to recognise the bias of the barristers to arrive at a fair
verdict, see if you can explain how Antony has coloured his account to
manipulate your emotions and show the conspirators in a bad light.

---

mantle cloak
the Nervii a fierce tribe in Gaul
who mounted a surprise ambush
against Caesar, but were repulsed
and slaughtered; this, Caesar's
most brilliant military achievement,
caused great rejoicing in Rome

Then make a ring about the corpse of Caesar
And let me show you him that made the will.   150
Shall I descend? And will you give me leave?
ALL Come down.
2 PLEBEIAN Descend.
3 PLEBEIAN You shall have leave.
               [*Antony comes down from the pulpit*]
4 PLEBEIAN A ring, stand round.   155
1 PLEBEIAN Stand from the hearse, stand from the body.
2 PLEBEIAN Room for Antony, most noble Antony.
ANTONY Nay, press not so upon me, stand far off.
ALL Stand back! Room, bear back!
ANTONY If you have tears, prepare to shed them now.   160
          You all do know this mantle. I remember
          The first time ever Caesar put it on,
          'Twas on a summer's evening, in his tent,
          That day he overcame the Nervii.
          Look, in this place ran Cassius' dagger through;   165
          See what a rent the envious Casca made;
          Through this the well-belovèd Brutus stabbed,
          And as he plucked his cursèd steel away,
          Mark how the blood of Caesar followed it,
          As rushing out of doors to be resolved   170
          If Brutus so unkindly knocked or no,
          For Brutus, as you know, was Caesar's angel.
          Judge, O you gods, how dearly Caesar loved him!
          This was the most unkindest cut of all.
          For when the noble Caesar saw him stab,   175
          Ingratitude, more strong than traitors' arms,
          Quite vanquished him. Then burst his mighty heart,
          And, in his mantle muffling up his face,
          Even at the base of Pompey's statue
          (Which all the while ran blood) great Caesar fell.   180
          O, what a fall was there, my countrymen!
          Then I, and you, and all of us fell down,
          Whilst bloody treason flourished over us.
          O, now you weep, and I perceive you feel
          The dint of pity. These are gracious drops.   185

There are cries of grief when Antony displays the body. When he praises Brutus' oratory over his own, the crowd move to attack the conspirators.

1 Echoes in the market-place (in groups of four)

Antony finishes here with an explosion of verbal fireworks. Divide lines 214–20 between pairs, one playing Antony and the other an echo that picks up words and sounds which would reverberate through the market-place. Together, decide which words to emphasise for maximum effect. Finally, put the passage together and run it through as a group.

2 Blaming conspirators (in groups of four to five)

Brutus let Antony speak on the condition 'You shall not in your funeral speech blame us (3.1.245)'.

Imagine that by line 220 the conspirators have found out how Antony has roused the people, and send in a force to arrest him and disperse the crowd.

Organise your group into lawyers for the prosecution and the defence at Antony's trial. The prosecution must prove that he did blame the conspirators, the defence that he did not. Both sides must look very closely at the language of the speech.

When you have prepared your arguments, join up with another group, choose a judge, lawyers and a jury and run the trial for fifteen minutes or so. Finally, get the jury to sift the evidence and arrive at a verdict.

3 Orators ancient and modern

You have now heard the oratory of Murellus, Cassius, Caesar, Brutus and Antony. Find ten typical lines from each or some and jot down thoughts about their styles.

While you study *Julius Caesar*, watch public figures on television and see if they are like the orators in the play. You could even rewrite and deliver a speech from the play in the style and manner of a well-known modern-day speaker!

vesture clothing

Kind souls, what weep you when you but behold
Our Caesar's vesture wounded? Look you here,
Here is himself, marred as you see with traitors.
1 PLEBEIAN O piteous spectacle!
2 PLEBEIAN O noble Caesar!   190
3 PLEBEIAN O woeful day!
4 PLEBEIAN O traitors, villains!
1 PLEBEIAN O most bloody sight!
2 PLEBEIAN We will be revenged!
ALL Revenge! About! Seek! Burn! Fire! Kill!   195
        Slay! Let not a traitor live!
ANTONY Stay, countrymen.
1 PLEBEIAN Peace there, hear the noble Antony.
2 PLEBEIAN We'll hear him, we'll follow him, we'll die with him.
ANTONY Good friends, sweet friends, let me not stir you up   200
        To such a sudden flood of mutiny.
        They that have done this deed are honourable.
        What private griefs they have, alas, I know not,
        That made them do it. They are wise and honourable,
        And will no doubt with reasons answer you.   205
        I come not, friends, to steal away your hearts.
        I am no orator, as Brutus is,
        But – as you know me all – a plain blunt man
        That love my friend, and that they know full well
        That gave me public leave to speak of him.   210
        For I have neither wit, nor words, nor worth,
        Action, nor utterance, nor the power of speech
        To stir men's blood. I only speak right on.
        I tell you that which you yourselves do know,
        Show you sweet Caesar's wounds, poor, poor, dumb mouths,   215
        And bid them speak for me. But were I Brutus,
        And Brutus Antony, there were an Antony
        Would ruffle up your spirits and put a tongue
        In every wound of Caesar, that should move
        The stones of Rome to rise and mutiny.   220
ALL We'll mutiny.
1 PLEBEIAN   We'll burn the house of Brutus.
3 PLEBEIAN Away then, come, seek the conspirators.

Antony reveals how much Caesar's will left to the people. They swear vengeance on the conspirators and leave. Alone, Antony confides his satisfaction. Octavius' arrival is announced.

---

1 The Caesar Garden

From the Renaissance onwards, gardens often had symbolic meanings and patterns. A Paradise Garden was criss-crossed by paths to symbolise the rivers of Eden. In the eighteenth century, the trees of Blenheim Palace were planted in the formation of the Duke of Marlborough's troops at his most famous battle. Ideas for ingenious garden features were the fashion: water displays, statues, even machines to make magical noises!

A trip up the Thames in 1600 let you glimpse the gardens of the wealthy that stretched from St Pauls to Westminster (see the London map pages 172–3), but as yet there were no public gardens. London's first was planned for Moorfields, just north of the City wall, and work started six years later. So the bequest of Caesar's gardens (lines 237–41) touched on a subject topical to Shakespeare's audience.

2 A Caesar memorial

Design a fantastic layout or feature which will celebrate the life of your benefactor, Caesar. It is to be installed in the newly bequested gardens. Do not let your imagination be hindered by practicalities!

Work individually or in a group as a design consultancy. Present your ideas very fully worked or as a series of sketches with explanation. Use the play to give you ideas: Antony's eulogies (3.1), the dream (2.2), even Cassius' reference to him as Colossus, storm, fire, etc. (1.1 and 2). The 'monument' on page 179 may suggest a garden feature.

---

drachmaes silver coins; difficult to assess their value – what could you 'buy' a crowd with today?

arbours lawns, orchards and cultivated gardens
forms benches

ANTONY Yet hear me, countrymen, yet hear me speak.

ALL Peace ho, hear Antony, most noble Antony!

ANTONY Why, friends, you go to do you know not what.   225
              Wherein hath Caesar thus deserved your loves?
              Alas, you know not! I must tell you then:
              You have forgot the will I told you of.

ALL Most true. The will, let's stay and hear the will!

ANTONY Here is the will, and under Caesar's seal: 230
              To every Roman citizen he gives,
              To every several man, seventy-five drachmaes.

2 PLEBEIAN Most noble Caesar, we'll revenge his death!

3 PLEBEIAN O royal Caesar!

ANTONY Hear me with patience.   235

ALL Peace ho!

ANTONY Moreover, he hath left you all his walks,
              His private arbours and new-planted orchards,
              On this side Tiber; he hath left them you,
              And to your heirs for ever – common pleasures,   240
              To walk abroad and recreate yourselves.
              Here was a Caesar! When comes such another?

1 PLEBEIAN Never, never! Come, away, away!
              We'll burn his body in the holy place
              And with the brands fire the traitors' houses.   245
              Take up the body.

2 PLEBEIAN Go fetch fire!

3 PLEBEIAN Pluck down benches!

4 PLEBEIAN Pluck down forms, windows, anything!

                         Exeunt Plebeians [with the body]

ANTONY Now let it work. Mischief, thou art afoot,   250
              Take thou what course thou wilt!

              Enter SERVANT

                     How now, fellow?

SERVANT Sir, Octavius is already come to Rome.

ANTONY Where is he?

SERVANT He and Lepidus are at Caesar's house.

ANTONY And thither will I straight to visit him.   255

Octavius' servant reports that Brutus and Cassius have fled Rome.
Cinna the poet is interrogated by the plebeians. Going where?
Caesar's funeral. Friend or enemy? Friend.

---

1 Antony overheard (in groups of three to five)

Your production company, in a major television series, is to re-appraise Mark Antony's life and career some years after his death. In an interview, Octavius' and Antony's servants tell us they overheard what Antony said just before they entered at 3.1.276 and 3.2.252.

Write a script for the presenter to read after his interview with the servants. Your script should show how this revelation makes us re-examine everything Antony said or did after the assassination. It should also sum up this episode of Antony's life.

2 The fate of a conspirator (in pairs)

Brutus and Cassius escape. Other conspirators may not be so lucky. We hear no account of them.

Devise a fate which fits one of the other conspirators – 3.3 may give you ideas. You can act it out or write it as a newspaper article or a short story.

3 Arguing with the director again! (in groups of four)

This (3.3) is another scene which the director wants to cut (see 2.3 and 4). Again, the actors want to keep it. Both sides must have a good case. Argue for cutting or inclusion.

---

are rid have ridden
bear me a bang get a blow from
  me

He comes upon a wish. Fortune is merry,
And in this mood will give us anything.
SERVANT I heard him say Brutus and Cassius
Are rid like madmen through the gates of Rome.
ANTONY Belike they had some notice of the people,   260
How I had moved them. Bring me to Octavius.

Exeunt

ACT 3   SCENE 3
Rome   A street

Enter CINNA THE POET, and after him the PLEBEIANS

CINNA THE POET I dreamt tonight that I did feast with Caesar,
And things unluckily charge my fantasy.
I have no will to wander forth of doors,
Yet something leads me forth.
1 PLEBEIAN What is your name?   5
2 PLEBEIAN Whither are you going?
3 PLEBEIAN Where do you dwell?
4 PLEBEIAN Are you a married man or a bachelor?
2 PLEBEIAN Answer every man directly.
1 PLEBEIAN Ay, and briefly.   10
4 PLEBEIAN Ay, and wisely.
3 PLEBEIAN Ay, and truly, you were best.
CINNA THE POET What is my name? Whither am I going? Where do I
    dwell? Am I a married man or a bachelor? Then to answer every man
    directly and briefly, wisely and truly. Wisely I say I am a bachelor.   15
2 PLEBEIAN That's as much as to say they are fools that marry. You'll
    bear me a bang for that, I fear. Proceed directly.
CINNA THE POET Directly I am going to Caesar's funeral.
1 PLEBEIAN As a friend or an enemy?
CINNA THE POET As a friend.   20
2 PLEBEIAN That matter is answered directly.
4 PLEBEIAN For your dwelling – briefly.
CINNA THE POET Briefly, I dwell by the Capitol.
3 PLEBEIAN Your name, sir, truly.

Hearing his name, the Commoners accuse Cinna of conspiracy; he protests he's a poet. They drag him off anyway, intending to burn the conspirators' houses.

---

1 Plebeians remember (in groups of eight)

Before and during the Second World War, many Germans were incited by Hitler's oratory. They became involved in acts of persecution which they later regretted.

Four of you are Plebeians 1–4 in old age, the other four a group of primary schoolchildren who are taping senior citizens' reminiscences about events surrounding Caesar's assassination. Plebeians describe the influence of Antony's oratory very fully, as well as how they now feel about their deeds that night. The schoolchildren sharpen their memories with searching and detailed questions. Among other things, they want to know what happened to Cinna the poet – and why.

Royal Shakespeare Company, 1972. The death of Cinna the poet.

CINNA THE POET Truly, my name is Cinna.   25

1 PLEBEIAN Tear him to pieces, he's a conspirator.

CINNA THE POET I am Cinna the poet, I am Cinna the poet.

4 PLEBEIAN Tear him for his bad verses, tear him for his bad verses.

CINNA THE POET I am not Cinna the conspirator.

4 PLEBEIAN It is no matter, his name's Cinna. Pluck but his name out of   30
his heart and turn him going.

3 PLEBEIAN Tear him, tear him! Come, brands ho, firebrands! To
Brutus', to Cassius', burn all! Some to Decius' house, and some to
Casca's, some to Ligarius'! Away, go!

Exeunt all the Plebeians [forcing out Cinna]

| Pompey | Julius Caesar | Mark Antony |

| Octavius Caesar | Lepidus | Brutus |

The Triumvirate (Antony, Octavius and Lepidus) organise a purge
which includes family relatives. Antony shows contempt for Lepidus
in his absence. Octavius defends him.

1 What's the offence?

Reasons have to be given for a purge even in a police state. Write, in precise legal language, the Triumvirate's charge against conspirators and their sympathisers.

2 Gaining status (in groups of five or six)

You may have listened to or taken part in a conversation where what is said becomes unimportant because people only want to gain status and put each other down. They are trying to score points against each other.

Three of you read the parts of the triumvirs, Antony, Octavius and Lepidus. The others are a panel of judges who award points out of ten when one triumvir 'scores' over another. Points can also be taken away for loss of status!

First, look over the whole scene individually and decide where points are scored and how many. Then play the whole scene, with the triumvirs breaking off to claim points. Everybody can argue about points, but the panel's decision is final.

Lastly, put the scene on tape. When you play it back, listen to see if the voices score the points they should.

---

pricked marked
cut off some charge in
  legacies pay our expenses in
  money from Caesar's will
threefold world Europe, Africa
  and Asia (modern-day Turkey,
  Iran and Iraq); rule over the

Empire was divided between three
  men: the Triumvirate
voice side
proscription death penalty; 300
  out of 900 senators were executed,
  and 2,000 equites or 'aristocrats'
divers various

ACT 4   SCENE 1
Rome

Enter ANTONY, OCTAVIUS, and LEPIDUS

ANTONY These many then shall die, their names are pricked.

OCTAVIUS Your brother too must die; consent you, Lepidus?

LEPIDUS I do consent.

OCTAVIUS   Prick him down, Antony.

LEPIDUS Upon condition Publius shall not live,
       Who is your sister's son, Mark Antony.   5

ANTONY He shall not live – look, with a spot I damn him.
       But, Lepidus, go you to Caesar's house,
       Fetch the will hither, and we shall determine
       How to cut off some charge in legacies.

LEPIDUS What, shall I find you here?   10

OCTAVIUS Or here or at the Capitol.

                            Exit Lepidus

ANTONY This is a slight, unmeritable man,
       Meet to be sent on errands; is it fit,
       The threefold world divided, he should stand
       One of the three to share it?

OCTAVIUS   So you thought him   15
       And took his voice who should be pricked to die
       In our black sentence and proscription.

ANTONY Octavius, I have seen more days than you,
       And though we lay these honours on this man
       To ease ourselves of divers slanderous loads,   20
       He shall but bear them as the ass bears gold,
       To groan and sweat under the business,
       Either led or driven, as we point the way;
       And having brought our treasure where we will,
       Then take we down his load and turn him off   25
       (Like to the empty ass) to shake his ears
       And graze in commons.

OCTAVIUS   You may do your will,
       But he's a tried and valiant soldier.

Antony compares Lepidus to his horse. He and Octavius prepare for war against Brutus and Cassius. In the next scene, Brutus asks Pindarus to bring his master Cassius to discuss Cassius' suspected misdeeds.

1 Lepidus, the third triumvir (in groups of three)

Lines 12–40 describe Lepidus, but Antony and Octavius disagree about him and so leave the actor free to decide his character. Rotating the parts, play Lepidus in lines 1–11 in as many ways as you can, experimenting with quite opposite interpretations. Have him say the thoughts in his head as he exits. Talk together about how the portrayal of Lepidus will influence an audience's viewpoint of Antony and Octavius.

If you have time, improvise a television interview with Lepidus outside the building.

2 Out with the 'in' crowd

Most people like to feel up to date. In lines 36–9, Antony says that Lepidus is always just behind the fashion or latest craze. Study the lines, then make up a person who wants to keep up but is always just behind. You could draw him or her and write a description underneath.

3 Recruiting in Asia (in two groups of up to five each)

When Cassius and Brutus return to the stage in 4.2 they have large armies raised in Asia (which, at that time, meant modern-day Turkey, Iraq and Iran).

Imagine one group of you are Republican recruiting officers who try to explain why Brutus and Cassius must defeat Antony and Octavius. The other group are Asians who challenge and ask questions. Assume that newspapers have kept them well informed!

---

provender food
wind turn
corporal physical
covert hidden

at the stake unable to move, like bears attacked by dogs at bear-baiting (see **Capitol**, pages 171–3)
ill bad

ANTONY So is my horse, Octavius, and for that
    I do appoint him store of provender.   30
    It is a creature that I teach to fight,
    To wind, to stop, to run directly on,
    His corporal motion governed by my spirit.
    And, in some taste, is Lepidus but so:
    He must be taught and trained and bid go forth,   35
    A barren-spirited fellow, one that feeds
    On objects, arts, and imitations,
    Which, out of use and staled by other men,
    Begin his fashion. Do not talk of him
    But as a property. And now, Octavius,   40
    Listen great things. Brutus and Cassius
    Are levying powers; we must straight make head.
    Therefore let our alliance be combined,
    Our best friends made, our means stretched,
    And let us presently go sit in counsel,   45
    How covert matters may be best disclosed
    And open perils surest answerèd.
OCTAVIUS Let us do so, for we are at the stake
    And bayed about with many enemies,
    And some that smile have in their hearts, I fear,   50
    Millions of mischiefs.

                    Exeunt

ACT 4   SCENE 2
Brutus' camp near Sardis in Asia

Drum. Enter BRUTUS, LUCILIUS, [Lucius,] *and the army. Titinius and*
PINDARUS *meet them*

BRUTUS Stand ho!
LUCILIUS Give the word ho, and stand!
BRUTUS What now, Lucilius, is Cassius near?
LUCILIUS He is at hand, and Pindarus is come
    To do you salutation from his master.   5
BRUTUS He greets me well. Your master, Pindarus,
    In his own change or by ill officers,
    Hath given me some worthy cause to wish
    Things done undone, but if he be at hand
    I shall be satisfied.

Lucilius, returned from Cassius, reports that Cassius is no longer as friendly as before. Cassius enters with his army and says Brutus has wronged him. Brutus urges him to speak quietly.

1 Army manoeuvres in the hall (in groups of three)

Stage directions call for two armies. Shakespeare's company was fifteen strong. One picture on page 110 shows the army as Shakespeare might have staged it; the other picture shows a real Elizabethan army.

In your school it might be possible to have a large army on stage. As directors, look carefully at line 30. Plan how you could stage it in your school hall. Explore ideas about sound effects, costume, movement and number of actors. If you enjoy doing this, you could do the same for Act 5, Scenes 1 and 4. A thought: Notice how often horses are mentioned, from the start of Act 4.

2 Orchestrating the quarrel (in pairs)

Brutus' and Cassius' quarrel holds the stage up to line 162 in a scene of strong emotion that must be carefully 'orchestrated' by the actors. Too loud and it will exhaust the audience, too restrained and it could bore them.

Imagine you have a 'volume control' calibrated 1–10, where normal conversation registers 4. Talk together about the scene, suggesting volume levels at particular points. Remember a big climax could be silence, or intense emotion a whisper.

Finally, read the scene aloud so that you think it sounds 'right', which does not necessarily mean as you planned it!

instances signs (of friendship)
hot at hand keen to be off at first
low march a quiet marching drum beat
jades horses without spirit or stamina

Sardis this town was near Izmir in modern Turkey, about 850 miles from Rome
the horse the cavalry

PINDARUS   I do not doubt   10
           But that my noble master will appear
           Such as he is, full of regard and honour.
BRUTUS He is not doubted.
                    [*Brutus and Lucilius draw apart*]
                    A word, Lucilius,
           How he received you; let me be resolved.
LUCILIUS With courtesy and with respect enough,   15
           But not with such familiar instances,
           Nor with such free and friendly conference,
           As he hath used of old.
BRUTUS   Thou hast described
           A hot friend cooling. Ever note, Lucilius,
           When love begins to sicken and decay   20
           It useth an enforcèd ceremony.
           There are no tricks in plain and simple faith,
           But hollow men, like horses hot at hand,
           Make gallant show and promise of their mettle.
                    Low march within
           But when they should endure the bloody spur   25
           They fall their crests, and like deceitful jades
           Sink in the trial. Comes his army on?
LUCILIUS They mean this night in Sardis to be quartered.
           The greater part, the horse in general,
           Are come with Cassius.

                    Enter CASSIUS *and his powers*

BRUTUS   Hark, he is arrived.   30
           March gently on to meet him.
CASSIUS Stand ho!
BRUTUS Stand ho, speak the word along!
1 SOLDIER Stand!
2 SOLDIER Stand!   35
3 SOLDIER Stand!
CASSIUS Most noble brother, you have done me wrong.
BRUTUS Judge me, you gods! Wrong I mine enemies?
           And if not so, how should I wrong a brother?
CASSIUS Brutus, this sober form of yours hides wrongs,   40
           And when you do them –
BRUTUS   Cassius, be content,
           Speak your griefs softly, I do know you well.

Brutus and Cassius enter Brutus' tent for privacy. Inside, Brutus charges Cassius with greed and corruption. Cassius says that if such accusations came from anyone but Brutus he would kill them.

---

1 Canvas walls have ears (in groups of four)

Brutus' and Cassius' quarrel could decide the fate of the Republican cause. It can only succeed if they are allies. As two of you read aloud lines 1–123, the other two imagine you are Lucilius and Titinius on guard, listening through the tent's thin walls. Though ordered not to interrupt, whisper to each other about:

a when you feel it must come to a duel
b how they manage to avoid a duel
c when you think either of them gain or lose honour (see **Honour**, page 175).

2 Compromised (in two groups of three or four each)

You are leading members of a successful new political party. One group is a family firm of builders which contributes most of the funds. The other group is the rest of the party executive. All of you are close personal friends.

The executive has just learned that the family have been accused of using their influence as town councillors to land a massive building contract for an unpopular new shopping centre in their locality. When the news breaks, it will destroy the party's reputation for honesty. But the party needs the family's money and charismatic leadership in the forthcoming general election.

In your separate groups, talk over what is to be done. Then come together to thrash out the problem.

Afterwards, talk together about your improvisation and how it relates to Scene 4.

---

charges troops
nice tiny, trivial
mart market

Before the eyes of both our armies here –
Which should perceive nothing but love from us –
Let us not wrangle. Bid them move away.   45
Then in my tent, Cassius, enlarge your griefs
And I will give you audience.
CASSIUS   Pindarus,
Bid our commanders lead their charges off
A little from this ground.
BRUTUS   Lucius, do you the like, and let no man   50
Come to our tent till we have done our conference.
Let Lucilius and Titinius guard our door.
Exeunt [all but] Brutus and Cassius

ACT 4   SCENE 3
In Brutus' tent

CASSIUS   That you have wronged me doth appear in this:
You have condemned and noted Lucius Pella
For taking bribes here of the Sardians,
Wherein my letters, praying on his side,
Because I knew the man, was slighted off.   5
BRUTUS   You wronged yourself to write in such a case.
CASSIUS   In such a time as this it is not meet
That every nice offence should bear his comment.
BRUTUS   Let me tell you, Cassius, you yourself
Are much condemned to have an itching palm,   10
To sell and mart your offices for gold
To undeservers.
CASSIUS   I, an itching palm?
You know that you are Brutus that speaks this,
Or, by the gods, this speech were else your last.
BRUTUS   The name of Cassius honours this corruption,   15
And chastisement doth therefore hide his head.
CASSIUS   Chastisement?
BRUTUS   Remember March, the Ides of March remember:
Did not great Julius bleed for justice' sake?

Caesar was killed to stamp out corruption, says Brutus. Cassius claims greater experience as a soldier. Brutus scorns Cassius' bad temper.

1 Management styles (in groups of four)

Plutarch says that 'when Caesar returned out of Africa and progressed up and down Italy, the things that pleased him best to see were the cities under Brutus' charge and government'.

You are a firm of management consultants who have been asked to write a report on the contrasting management styles of Cassius and Brutus.

- You can use the whole scene as evidence or just the opposite page.
- Talk together about how the two leaders deal with each other.
- How would they manage an army or city of many thousands?
- Interview another group posing as workers under the two leaders.

2 Quarrelling rhythms (in pairs or groups of three)

The rhythms of speech in this scene suggest the strength or weakness of the characters as much as what is said.

Read carefully from 'I am a soldier, I' (line 30) to line 42. You will find many short and broken lines. Where the pauses fall will be crucial to the balance between Brutus and Cassius. Try reading it in different ways and decide which sounds right.

sell the mighty space of our large honours profit by our noble position. When Essex fell from favour in 1599, Elizabeth I took away his monopoly in the sweet wine trade. It ruined him. (Honourable court positions were in themselves worthless, but lucrative because they enabled the holder to sell trade licences at great profit)

be a dog and bay the moon the watchdog barks because it believes its shadow, cast by the moon, is another dog
choler bad temper
testy irritable

What villain touched his body, that did stab 20
And not for justice? What, shall one of us,
That struck the foremost man of all this world,
But for supporting robbers, shall we now
Contaminate our fingers with base bribes
And sell the mighty space of our large honours 25
For so much trash as may be graspèd thus?
I had rather be a dog and bay the moon
Than such a Roman.
CASSIUS   Brutus, bait not me,
I'll not endure it. You forget yourself
To hedge me in. I am a soldier, I, 30
Older in practice, abler than yourself
To make conditions.
BRUTUS   Go to, you are not, Cassius!
CASSIUS I am.
BRUTUS I say you are not.
CASSIUS Urge me no more, I shall forget myself. 35
Have mind upon your health, tempt me no farther!
BRUTUS Away, slight man!
CASSIUS Is't possible?
BRUTUS   Hear me, for I will speak.
Must I give way and room to your rash choler?
Shall I be frighted when a madman stares? 40
CASSIUS O ye gods, ye gods, must I endure all this?
BRUTUS All this? Ay, more. Fret till your proud heart break.
Go show your slaves how choleric you are,
And make your bondmen tremble. Must I budge?
Must I observe you? Must I stand and crouch 45
Under your testy humour? By the gods,
You shall digest the venom of your spleen
Though it do split you. For, from this day forth,
I'll use you for my mirth, yea, for my laughter,
When you are waspish.
CASSIUS   Is it come to this? 50
BRUTUS You say you are a better soldier:
Let it appear so, make your vaunting true
And it shall please me well. For mine own part
I shall be glad to learn of noble men.

Brutus shrugs off Cassius' temper but is angry that Cassius refused him gold for his troops. Cassius says friends should not magnify each other's faults.

---

1 Money!

Roman generals owned their armies and paid them out of their own pockets, but the loot of foreign conquest could be vastly profitable and buy political influence at home.

Generals minted their own coins with their own 'heads and tails' on them (see page 109 for examples of heads). Like today's coins, money carried designs which symbolised something important to those who used it. This Italian coin of 90 BC shows the Italian lion goring the Roman wolf at a time when Italy and Rome were at war.

2 Different attitudes

Study lines 69–82 and lines 100–5 to find Brutus and Cassius describing their attitude to money, and 3.2.120–50 and 4.1.7–27 for Antony's attitude.

3 Design a coin (in groups of three or four)

As a design consultancy, come up with a series of designs for coin 'tails' for Brutus or Cassius. Your designs should make the soldiers think what they are fighting for when they get paid.

Write a short explanation beside each design, which can of course be much larger than the actual coins would be.

---

durst dared
drachmaes silver coins
rived split

CASSIUS You wrong me every way, you wrong me, Brutus.   55
          I said an elder soldier, not a better.
          Did I say 'better'?
BRUTUS   If you did, I care not.
CASSIUS When Caesar lived, he durst not thus have moved me.
BRUTUS Peace, peace, you durst not so have tempted him.
CASSIUS I durst not?   60
BRUTUS No.
CASSIUS What? Durst not tempt him?
BRUTUS   For your life you durst not.
CASSIUS Do not presume too much upon my love,
          I may do that I shall be sorry for.
BRUTUS You have done that you should be sorry for.   65
          There is no terror, Cassius, in your threats,
          For I am armed so strong in honesty
          That they pass by me as the idle wind,
          Which I respect not. I did send to you
          For certain sums of gold, which you denied me,   70
          For I can raise no money by vile means.
          By heaven, I had rather coin my heart
          And drop my blood for drachmaes than to wring
          From the hard hands of peasants their vile trash
          By any indirection. I did send   75
          To you for gold to pay my legions,
          Which you denied me. Was that done like Cassius?
          Should I have answered Caius Cassius so?
          When Marcus Brutus grows so covetous
          To lock such rascal counters from his friends,   80
          Be ready, gods, with all your thunderbolts,
          Dash him to pieces!
CASSIUS   I denied you not.
BRUTUS You did.
CASSIUS I did not. He was but a fool that brought
          My answer back. Brutus hath rived my heart.   85
          A friend should bear his friend's infirmities,
          But Brutus makes mine greater than they are.
BRUTUS I do not, till you practise them on me.

Stung by Brutus' criticism, Cassius asks Brutus to kill him. Brutus relents, admits blame himself and resolves to ignore Cassius' temper in future.

---

1 A notable friendship (in groups of three or four)

After Cassius' outburst at lines 93–107, Brutus and Cassius suddenly become, and remain, firm friends.

The cultivation of friendship was an all-important duty in the Ancient World. In the year of Caesar's death, Cicero wrote in his essay *Of Friendship*:

> Take away the bond of kindly feeling from the world, and no house or city can stand. Even the fields will no longer be cultivated. If that sounds exaggerated, consider the opposite state of affairs: note the disasters that come from dissension and enmity. When there is internal hatred and division, no home or country in the world is strong enough to avoid destruction.

At the end of this scene, Brutus is reading a book. Imagine he was reading the passage above. He is full of sadness as Cicero has just been killed in the purge. It spurs him on to confide his thoughts in a soliloquy at line 275, which you can write.

As you read through, gather material for your soliloquy from the rest of the scene. Brutus shows true Stoic self control as he and the generals mull over news from Rome, but alone he can ponder aloud the whole enterprise he undertook with Cassius.

Research together, but write individually. Concentrate your ideas into poetry, but not necessarily Shakespearean verse. Dramatic poetry should be condensed and fast moving – forty lines maximum.

Olympus a Greek mountain, home of the gods
conned by rote learned by heart
Pluto's mine infinite wealth (Cassius runs two names together: Plutus, a fabulously rich man, and Pluto, wealthy king of the underworld)

beest are
much enforcèd when struck violently

CASSIUS You love me not.
BRUTUS   I do not like your faults.
CASSIUS A friendly eye could never see such faults.   90
BRUTUS A flatterer's would not, though they do appear
         As huge as high Olympus.
CASSIUS Come, Antony, and young Octavius, come,
         Revenge yourselves alone on Cassius,
         For Cassius is a-weary of the world: 95
         Hated by one he loves, braved by his brother,
         Checked like a bondman, all his faults observed,
         Set in a notebook, learned, and conned by rote,
         To cast into my teeth. O, I could weep
         My spirit from mine eyes! There is my dagger   100
         And here my naked breast: within, a heart
         Dearer than Pluto's mine, richer than gold.
         If that thou beest a Roman take it forth,
         I that denied thee gold will give my heart:
         Strike as thou didst at Caesar. For I know   105
         When thou didst hate him worst thou loved'st him better
         Than ever thou loved'st Cassius.
BRUTUS   Sheathe your dagger.
         Be angry when you will, it shall have scope;
         Do what you will, dishonour shall be humour.
         O Cassius, you are yokèd with a lamb   110
         That carries anger as the flint bears fire,
         Who, much enforcèd, shows a hasty spark
         And straight is cold again.
CASSIUS   Hath Cassius lived
         To be but mirth and laughter to his Brutus
         When grief and blood ill-tempered vexeth him?   115
BRUTUS When I spoke that, I was ill-tempered too.
CASSIUS Do you confess so much? Give me your hand.
BRUTUS And my heart too.
CASSIUS   O Brutus!
BRUTUS   What's the matter?
CASSIUS Have not you love enough to bear with me
         When that rash humour which my mother gave me   120
         Makes me forgetful?
BRUTUS   Yes, Cassius, and from henceforth
         When you are over-earnest with your Brutus,
         He'll think your mother chides, and leave you so.

A poet tries to intercede and reconcile Brutus and Cassius. With uncharacteristic fury, Brutus throws him out. Cassius is surprised. Brutus explains that his wife is dead.

1 Arguing with a Cynic (in pairs)

The Cynics, a group of Greek philosophers, taught that we should despise life. The most famous Cynic, Diogenes, lived in his coffin to show contempt for things of this earth. They were the hippies of the Ancient World.

Brutus loves philosophy, but is too keyed up at this moment to argue with the Poet. Later he might have time so improvise their conversation. Likely topics are Caesar's death, the war and the death of Portia. Your improvisation will give you a better understanding of Brutus' uncharacteristic rage at the Poet's interruption.

2 Should the Poet be cut? (in groups of six to eight)

The Poet interupts Brutus and Cassius' conversation in Plutarch's *History* in just this way, but Shakespeare could easily have left him out. Talk together about why he *was* included.

3 Portia's suicide note (in groups of three)

Plutarch says that Portia put burning coal in her mouth and choked to death. Talk together about what forced Portia to commit suicide and why she decided to do it this way.

a Write her suicide note.
b Exchange your note with another group and discuss the differences.

4 A covering letter

Someone must have sent Portia's suicide note to Brutus. Decide who it might have been and write the letter they would have sent to Brutus with Portia's note.

---

distract mad

Enter a POET, [LUCILIUS *and Titinius*]

POET Let me go in to see the generals.
　　　There is some grudge between 'em, 'tis not meet　　125
　　　They be alone.
LUCILIUS You shall not come to them.
POET Nothing but death shall stay me.
CASSIUS How now, what's the matter?
POET For shame, you generals, what do you mean?　　　130
　　　Love and be friends, as two such men should be,
　　　For I have seen more years, I'm sure, than ye.
CASSIUS Ha, ha, how vildly doth this cynic rhyme!
BRUTUS Get you hence, sirrah; saucy fellow, hence!
CASSIUS Bear with him, Brutus, 'tis his fashion.　　　135
BRUTUS I'll know his humour when he knows his time.
　　　What should the wars do with these jigging fools?
　　　Companion, hence!
CASSIUS　　　　　　　Away, away, be gone!

Exit Poet

BRUTUS Lucilius and Titinius, bid the commanders
　　　Prepare to lodge their companies tonight.　　　140
CASSIUS And come yourselves, and bring Messala with you
　　　Immediately to us.

[Exeunt Lucilius and Titinius]

BRUTUS *[To Lucius within]*　　Lucius, a bowl of wine!
CASSIUS I did not think you could have been so angry.
BRUTUS O Cassius, I am sick of many griefs.
CASSIUS Of your philosophy you make no use　　　145
　　　If you give place to accidental evils.
BRUTUS No man bears sorrow better. Portia is dead.
CASSIUS Ha? Portia?
BRUTUS She is dead.
CASSIUS How scaped I killing when I crossed you so?　　150
　　　O insupportable and touching loss!
　　　Upon what sickness?
BRUTUS　　　　　　　Impatient of my absence,
　　　And grief that young Octavius with Mark Antony
　　　Have made themselves so strong – for with her death
　　　That tidings came. With this she fell distract　　155
　　　And, her attendants absent, swallowed fire.

Julius Caesar

Reconciled, Brutus and Cassius drink wine. Titinius and Messala enter to report that the Triumvirate have executed Cicero and 100 other senators, and now approach Philippi.

1 Wine and tapers (in groups of three)

Colonising Romans 'civilised' their conquered subjects by encouraging them to cultivate vineyards. Wine growing is an art of peace and wine still has symbolic or religious meanings. Many customs and rituals use wine or alcohol.

In the gathering darkness suggested by Lucius' tapers, Brutus and Cassius drain their bowl of wine. As he would at home, Lucius brings hospitality to Cassius even though they are in a tent 850 miles from Rome and Portia is dead.

Read and mime the actions from Lucius' entrance to his exit (lines 158–62). These five lines might take quite a long time to act out on stage. Feel your way into the characters' minds as you act. Compare their thoughts when you have finished.

Sum up the experience in a poem.

2 The bringer of bad news (in groups of four)

No subject ever wants to be the bringer of bad news to a ruler, yet a wise ruler values those who are frank.

a Hold a conversation between Messala and Titinius about how to break the news of Portia to Brutus, then act out lines 181–97, and finally talk together about Brutus' reaction, after you have left the tent.

b Lines 181–97 are often cut because they seem to repeat the breaking of news about Portia's death. As the four actors in this scene, talk together about how to retain these lines and play them convincingly. Then decide whether or not to cut them.

Philippi (pronounced fye-lip-eye) where the Republicans were defeated in 42 BC on the coast of Eastern Greece near Thasos; in reality Sardis and Philippi were 260 miles and a sea journey apart

proscription death penalty

128

CASSIUS And died so?
BRUTUS   Even so.
CASSIUS   O ye immortal gods!

Enter BOY [LUCIUS] *with wine and tapers*

BRUTUS Speak no more of her. Give me a bowl of wine.
          In this I bury all unkindness, Cassius.   *Drinks*
CASSIUS My heart is thirsty for that noble pledge.   160
          Fill, Lucius, till the wine o'erswell the cup,
          I cannot drink too much of Brutus' love.   [*Drinks*]
                                                    [*Exit Lucius*]

Enter TITINIUS *and* MESSALA

BRUTUS Come in, Titinius; welcome, good Messala.
          Now sit we close about this taper here
          And call in question our necessities.   165
CASSIUS Portia, art thou gone?
BRUTUS   No more, I pray you.
          Messala, I have here receivèd letters
          That young Octavius and Mark Antony
          Come down upon us with a mighty power,
          Bending their expedition toward Philippi.   170
MESSALA Myself have letters of the selfsame tenor.
BRUTUS With what addition?
MESSALA That by proscription and bills of outlawry
          Octavius, Antony, and Lepidus
          Have put to death an hundred senators.   175
BRUTUS Therein our letters do not well agree:
          Mine speak of seventy senators that died
          By their proscriptions, Cicero being one.
CASSIUS Cicero one?
MESSALA   Cicero is dead,
          And by that order of proscription.   180
          Had you your letters from your wife, my lord?
BRUTUS No, Messala.
MESSALA Nor nothing in your letters writ of her?
BRUTUS Nothing, Messala.
MESSALA   That, methinks, is strange.

Brutus philosophically receives news of Portia's death, then turns to military tactics. Take battle to the enemy, he says. Let battle come to us, says Cassius. Brutus insists his plan is best.

1 The Free Rome Broadcasting Network
(in groups of up to six)

Republicans at home and in exile keep in close touch. Those at home keep the Republican flame burning among the people. Those abroad raise armies to recapture Rome. Imagine there is a broadcasting network to keep all Republicans informed.

Put together a radio or television programme which emphasises the horrors of Triumvirate rule, yet celebrates Republican achievement and gives heart to those who carry on the struggle. Use excerpts from the play as tape recordings or newsreel, and invent interviews with leading Republicans.

2 Good friends – good generals? (in groups of three)

Titinius knows, from the start of the scene, that Brutus and Cassius have had a terrific quarrel. Bring Titinius, Messala and Lucilius together to talk over the change Titinius found in the two men and guess at reasons for it. Then also wonder if the right military tactic has been chosen for tomorrow's battle. Set your conversation in the officers' mess the following morning.

3 A tide in the affairs of men (in groups of three or four)

In the days of sail power and undredged estuaries, trading ships often had to wait for the right wind and tide. Too long a wait and the cargo might lose its value, especially if it was perishable. Sail at the wrong time and the ship could be wrecked. Either way investors would lose money on the venture.

Talk together about whether what Brutus says in lines 218–24 is true of life as you know it. Make a short improvisation that shows him to be right or wrong.

---

in art if I pretend
**do stand but in a forced
  affection** show friendship that is
  not spontaneous

BRUTUS Why ask you? Hear you aught of her in yours?   185
MESSALA No, my lord.
BRUTUS Now as you are a Roman tell me true.
MESSALA Then like a Roman bear the truth I tell,
    For certain she is dead, and by strange manner.
BRUTUS Why, farewell, Portia. We must die, Messala.   190
    With meditating that she must die once,
    I have the patience to endure it now.
MESSALA Even so, great men great losses should endure.
CASSIUS I have as much of this in art as you,
    But yet my nature could not bear it so.   195
BRUTUS Well, to our work alive. What do you think
    Of marching to Philippi presently?
CASSIUS I do not think it good.
BRUTUS   Your reason?
CASSIUS   This it is:
    'Tis better that the enemy seek us,
    So shall he waste his means, weary his soldiers,   200
    Doing himself offence, whilst we, lying still,
    Are full of rest, defence, and nimbleness.
BRUTUS Good reasons must of force give place to better:
    The people 'twixt Philippi and this ground
    Do stand but in a forced affection,   205
    For they have grudged us contribution.
    The enemy, marching along by them,
    By them shall make a fuller number up,
    Come on refreshed, new added, and encouraged,
    From which advantage shall we cut him off   210
    If at Philippi we do face him there,
    These people at our back.
CASSIUS   Hear me, good brother.
BRUTUS Under your pardon. You must note beside
    That we have tried the utmost of our friends,
    Our legions are brimful, our cause is ripe;   215
    The enemy increaseth every day,
    We, at the height, are ready to decline.
    There is a tide in the affairs of men
    Which, taken at the flood, leads on to fortune;
    Omitted, all the voyage of their life   220
    Is bound in shallows and in miseries.

Cassius agrees to go to the enemy at Philippi. After a harmonious leave-taking, Brutus is left to sleep. He asks Lucius for music.

---

1 The last night of the Roman Republic

'The deep of night is crept upon our talk', says Brutus. Capture the mood of the scene in a poem of your own, from the entry of Lucius (line 158) either to the departure of the generals (line 238), or to the disappearance of the ghost (line 286). Start or end each verse with this chorus:

> The last night of the Roman Republic
> Five centuries old
> Tapers flickered in Brutus' tent
> And darkness fell and fell.

Think your way into Brutus' hopes, fears, memories, sadness, bravery, friendship . . . everything that goes on under the calm surface.

Change the chorus if you wish or cut it altogether.

2 Calm after the storm (in groups of four)

Lines 30–42 of this scene (page 121) were full of short and broken lines. Here, lines 229–40 are much more regular, though nearly all shared. Read both sets of lines with careful regard for the rhythm. Talk together about the contrasting effects.

3 Strictly for the record (in two pairs)

At 5.1.69, Brutus talks confidentially to Lucilius, and Cassius to Messala. Of those who survive the battle, these two are best qualified to write a biographical memoir of the leader's last days.

Two persons as Lucilius and Messala think of questions to ask the two leaders about their reconciliation. The other pair, as Brutus and Cassius re-read the scene, as if going over it in memory to prepare for their confidential records.

Then carry out the interview.

On such a full sea are we now afloat,
And we must take the current when it serves
Or lose our ventures.

CASSIUS   Then with your will go on,
We'll along ourselves and meet them at Philippi.   225

BRUTUS The deep of night is crept upon our talk,
And nature must obey necessity,
Which we will niggard with a little rest.
There is no more to say?

CASSIUS   No more. Good night.
Early tomorrow will we rise and hence.   230

BRUTUS Lucius!

Enter LUCIUS

My gown.

                                             [Exit Lucius]

Farewell, good Messala.
Good night, Titinius. Noble, noble Cassius,
Good night and good repose.

CASSIUS   O my dear brother!
This was an ill beginning of the night.
Never come such division 'tween our souls!   235
Let it not, Brutus.

Enter LUCIUS *with the gown*

BRUTUS   Everything is well.

CASSIUS Good night, my lord.

BRUTUS   Good night, good brother.

TITINIUS AND MESSALA Good night, Lord Brutus.

BRUTUS   Farewell every one.
                         Exeunt [Cassius, Titinius, Messala]
Give me the gown. Where is thy instrument?

LUCIUS Here in the tent.

BRUTUS   What, thou speak'st drowsily.   240
Poor knave, I blame thee not, thou art o'erwatched.
Call Claudio and some other of my men,
I'll have them sleep on cushions in my tent.

LUCIUS Varrus and Claudio!

Varrus and Claudio are summoned to sleep in Brutus' tent. Lucius plays music but falls asleep. While Brutus reads, the ghost of Caesar enters.

---

1 History above and below stairs (in groups of five to eight)

Servants often provide biographical detail about the private lives of historical figures. In this act, Shakespeare shows how all the leaders behave in private: Antony, Octavius, Brutus and Cassius.

Imagine the historian Plutarch and his researchers have found the personal attendants on the four leaders in old age. They are about to interview them.

Divide into 'historians' and 'servants'. While the servants refresh their memories about their masters (and perhaps read on, as Pindarus should) the historians prepare questions to ask. Typical ones might be: How did he treat his wife? How would he deal with a slave's petty theft? What kind of vehicle did he own? Build a picture of the leaders from both the play and your own imaginations.

2 Compose Lucius' song (in pairs)

No words or music survive for Lucius' song, so as musical directors you have to supply them. Think about the mood needed and the rightness of the words. Compose your own music or set your words to a tune you know already. Well-known tunes can be adapted by speeding them up or slowing them down.

3 A notable friendship

Now you have reached this point in your reading you will be able to complete the activity described on page 124.

Enter VARRUS *and* CLAUDIO

VARRUS Calls my lord?   245
BRUTUS I pray you, sirs, lie in my tent and sleep,
          It may be I shall raise you by and by
          On business to my brother Cassius.
VARRUS So please you, we will stand and watch your pleasure.
BRUTUS I will not have it so. Lie down, good sirs,   250
          It may be I shall otherwise bethink me.
                    [*Varrus and Claudio lie down*]
          Look, Lucius, here's the book I sought for so,
          I put it in the pocket of my gown.
LUCIUS I was sure your lordship did not give it me.
BRUTUS Bear with me, good boy, I am much forgetful.   255
          Canst thou hold up thy heavy eyes awhile
          And touch thy instrument a strain or two?
LUCIUS Ay, my lord, an't please you.
BRUTUS   It does, my boy.
          I trouble thee too much, but thou art willing.
LUCIUS It is my duty, sir.   260
BRUTUS I should not urge thy duty past thy might,
          I know young bloods look for a time of rest.
LUCIUS I have slept, my lord, already.
BRUTUS It was well done and thou shalt sleep again,
          I will not hold thee long. If I do live   265
          I will be good to thee.
                    Music, and a song
          This is a sleepy tune. O murd'rous slumber,
          Layest thou thy leaden mace upon my boy,
          That plays thee music? Gentle knave, good night,
          I will not do thee so much wrong to wake thee.   270
          If thou dost nod thou break'st thy instrument.
          I'll take it from thee and, good boy, good night.
          Let me see, let me see, is not the leaf turned down
          Where I left reading? Here it is, I think.

Enter the GHOST OF CAESAR

          How ill this taper burns! Ha, who comes here?   275

Promising a second appearance, the ghost disappears. Brutus wakes the
servants and orders immediate preparations for battle.

---

1 Caesar's ghost

Ghosts were highly significant for many Elizabethans. They believed
that ghosts could be good or bad, silent or talkative, truthful or
deceptive. Evil spirits could disguise themselves to mislead mortals. If
you knew how to talk to a ghost, you could gain valuable (or
misleading) information about the past, present or future. Shakespeare drew on this interest in his plays – see *Macbeth* Act 1, Scene 3,
and *Hamlet* Act 1, Scenes 4 and 5.

2 First appearance (in pairs)

Read or stage lines 273–88 as dramatically as you can.

3 Second appearance (in groups of six)

We learn that Brutus *did* see the ghost again (5.5.17–19), but the play
does not give us that scene. Improvise the ghost's second appearance.
Work in two groups: one group as Brutus and one as the ghost.

Brutus' group: think about how the ghost should be spoken to.
Prepare questions for Brutus to ask.

Ghost group: decide who the ghost is and what his motives are.
Anticipate Brutus' questions, and decide what information to give
him, and how to speak, straight or riddling.

Now play out the second appearance.

4 Actual appearance (in groups of four)

What does Caesar's ghost look like? Every director of the play must
decide what the audience will see: bloodstains? larger than life? a
floating head? Talk together about how you could present Caesar's
ghost in your production to make the greatest impression on the
audience.

5 'Some god, some angel, or some devil'

Write six more lines for Brutus, beginning 'If you are a god . . .'.

I think it is the weakness of mine eyes
That shapes this monstrous apparition.
It comes upon me. Art thou any thing?
Art thou some god, some angel, or some devil,
That mak'st my blood cold and my hair to stare?   280
Speak to me what thou art.
GHOST Thy evil spirit, Brutus.
BRUTUS   Why com'st thou?
GHOST To tell thee thou shalt see me at Philippi.
BRUTUS Well, then I shall see thee again?
GHOST Ay, at Philippi.   285
BRUTUS Why, I will see thee at Philippi then.

                                            [*Exit Ghost*]

Now I have taken heart thou vanishest.
Ill spirit, I would hold more talk with thee.
Boy, Lucius! Varrus! Claudio! Sirs, awake!
Claudio!   290
LUCIUS The strings, my lord, are false.
BRUTUS He thinks he still is at his instrument.
Lucius, awake!
LUCIUS My lord?
BRUTUS Didst thou dream, Lucius, that thou so cried'st out?   295
LUCIUS My lord, I do not know that I did cry.
BRUTUS Yes, that thou didst. Didst thou see anything?
LUCIUS Nothing, my lord.
BRUTUS Sleep again, Lucius. Sirrah Claudio!
[*To Varrus*] Fellow, thou, awake!   300
VARRUS My lord?
CLAUDIO My lord?
BRUTUS Why did you so cry out, sirs, in your sleep?
BOTH Did we, my lord?
BRUTUS   Ay. Saw you anything?
VARRUS No, my lord, I saw nothing.
CLAUDIO   Nor I, my lord.   305
BRUTUS Go and commend me to my brother Cassius.
Bid him set on his powers betimes before,
And we will follow.
BOTH   It shall be done, my lord.

                                            Exeunt

Octavius and Antony argue about why the enemy has come down to them, and both vie for leadership in the coming battle. Brutus and Cassius enter with their army.

---

1 Tony and Tavy's argy-bargy (in pairs)

Each time we have seen Antony and Octavius together they have argued. Both argue in different ways.

Make up an argument between two people today. It can be about anything you like. Decide beforehand who will argue like Antony and who like Octavius. See how quickly other people can guess which is which.

2 Right of the line (in two groups of four each)

According to Plutarch the battlefield of Philippi looked like this:

Antony (right)	Octavius (left)
v	v
Cassius (left)	Brutus (right)

The superior general always fought on the right of the line of battle: that's why lines 16–20 are so important. Shakespeare retains who fought whom, but leaves right and left open to directors of the play to decide. One of your groups consists of the Triumvirate leaders and the other the Republican leaders, with two military experts to arbitrate on each side. Hold frank discussions between the leaders as to who should fight on the right. Take into account military advantage, personal status and integrity, age and experience.

I am in their bosoms I know what they are thinking

exigent crisis
parley talks under truce

ACT 5   SCENE 1
The battlefield at Philippi in Greece

Enter OCTAVIUS, ANTONY, *and their army*

OCTAVIUS Now, Antony, our hopes are answerèd.
　　　　You said the enemy would not come down
　　　　But keep the hills and upper regions.
　　　　It proves not so: their battles are at hand,
　　　　They mean to warn us at Philippi here,　　　　　　5
　　　　Answering before we do demand of them.
ANTONY Tut, I am in their bosoms, and I know
　　　　Wherefore they do it. They could be content
　　　　To visit other places and come down
　　　　With fearful bravery, thinking by this face　　　　10
　　　　To fasten in our thoughts that they have courage.
　　　　But 'tis not so.

Enter a MESSENGER

MESSENGER　　　　　　Prepare you, generals,
　　　　The enemy comes on in gallant show,
　　　　Their bloody sign of battle is hung out,
　　　　And something to be done immediately.　　　　　15
ANTONY Octavius, lead your battle softly on
　　　　Upon the left hand of the even field.
OCTAVIUS Upon the right hand I, keep thou the left.
ANTONY Why do you cross me in this exigent?
OCTAVIUS I do not cross you, but I will do so.　　　　20
March

Drum. Enter BRUTUS, CASSIUS, *and their army;* [LUCILIUS, *Titinius*,
MESSALA, *and others*]

BRUTUS They stand and would have parley.
CASSIUS Stand fast, Titinius, we must out and talk.

*The generals parley, trading taunts and accusations. Octavius vows
vengeance for Caesar's death.*

---

1 Honour satisfied (in groups A and B of two or three each)

According to strict etiquette, a challenge that ends in a duel goes like
this:

- A insults B in front of witnesses (he gives B 'the lie')
- B accuses A of lying (giving the challenge and making a duel
  possible)
- A accepts the challenge
- They agree to fight and choose seconds.

If A really wants B to fight, he must make it impossible for B to
wriggle out of the insult by claiming A is misinformed, has got the
wrong person or whatever. A loses honour if his insult is proved to be
absurd. B must never appear to act from fear of A.

a In your improvisation, groups A and B represent opposing political
leaders (you could choose one you often see on television). Devise
insults which the other cannot wriggle out of with honour and
which, for an Elizabethan, must mean a duel. Then improvise the
four stages of the quarrel given above.

b When you have finished your improvisation, carefully work out
what each general is saying in this parley (lines 27–66). Give
individual scores to each general for the ingenuities of their insults.

2 Is battle inevitable? (in groups of four)

Can battle be avoided? Talk together about whether honourable
negotiation might be possible and desirable after line 58.

---

posture a difficult word:
  positioning? nature? imposture?

Hybla a Sicilian mountain famous
  for honey

OCTAVIUS Mark Antony, shall we give sign of battle?

ANTONY No, Caesar, we will answer on their charge.
　　　　Make forth, the generals would have some words.　　　　25

OCTAVIUS Stir not until the signal.

BRUTUS Words before blows; is it so, countrymen?

OCTAVIUS Not that we love words better, as you do.

BRUTUS Good words are better than bad strokes, Octavius.

ANTONY In your bad strokes, Brutus, you give good words.　　30
　　　　Witness the hole you made in Caesar's heart,
　　　　Crying, 'Long live, hail, Caesar!'

CASSIUS　　　　　　　　　　　　　　Antony,
　　　　The posture of your blows are yet unknown;
　　　　But for your words, they rob the Hybla bees
　　　　And leave them honeyless.

ANTONY　　　　　　　　　　　　Not stingless too?　　　　35

BRUTUS O yes, and soundless too,
　　　　For you have stolen their buzzing, Antony,
　　　　And very wisely threat before you sting.

ANTONY Villains! You did not so when your vile daggers
　　　　Hacked one another in the sides of Caesar.　　　　40
　　　　You showed your teeth like apes and fawned like hounds,
　　　　And bowed like bondmen, kissing Caesar's feet,
　　　　Whilst damnèd Casca, like a cur, behind
　　　　Struck Caesar on the neck. O you flatterers!

CASSIUS Flatterers? Now, Brutus, thank yourself.　　　　45
　　　　This tongue had not offended so today
　　　　If Cassius might have ruled.

OCTAVIUS Come, come, the cause. If arguing make us sweat,
　　　　The proof of it will turn to redder drops.
　　　　Look,　　　　　　　　　　　　　　　　　　　　　50
　　　　I draw a sword against conspirators;
　　　　When think you that the sword goes up again?
　　　　Never, till Caesar's three and thirty wounds
　　　　Be well avenged, or till another Caesar
　　　　Have added slaughter to the sword of traitors.　　　　55

BRUTUS Caesar, thou canst not die by traitors' hands
　　　　Unless thou bring'st them with thee.

OCTAVIUS　　　　　　　　　　　　　　So I hope.
　　　　I was not born to die on Brutus' sword.

Julius Caesar

*Cassius insults the triumvirs. Octavius defies him and the triumvirs leave
with their troops. Cassius, whose birthday it is, confides to Messala
his newfound respect for omens.*

1 Negotiations – or insults? (in groups of four)

Lines 21–68 make great theatre because they are filled with conflict.
If you have not already done so, take roles and read through or act out
the lines as expressively as possible.

2 Ending at the beginning

Cassius' life has come full circle (line 71). Draw a big circle with
Cassius' first and last day at 12 o'clock. Imagine how he spent his life
up to the start of the play. Make a pie chart of his fifty-five years,
labelling each section of it with detailed notes. Leave his death blank
until you know the manner of it!

3 Waiting to do battle

Before a big battle, soldiers often write down their thoughts in letters
or diaries. After Cassius' speech (lines 70–88), the parley and the
conversation last night, Messala has an in-depth knowledge of
Cassius' state of mind. Writing as Messala, see if you can pin down
your leader's state of mind on paper. Speculate whether it has been
sensed by the troops or affected their morale.

strain family
masker amateur actor in a masque,
an entertainment often brought on
at banquets at court; it was a
mixture between play, ballet and
opera with sumptuous costumes

on the hazard staked on a throw of
the dice
Epicurus a Greek philosopher who
held that our aim must be pleasure
in life because death is final
presage give knowledge of the
future

144

BRUTUS O, if thou wert the noblest of thy strain,
          Young man, thou couldst not die more honourable.   60
CASSIUS A peevish schoolboy, worthless of such honour,
          Joined with a masker and a reveller!
ANTONY Old Cassius still!
OCTAVIUS   Come, Antony, away!
          Defiance, traitors, hurl we in your teeth.
          If you dare fight today, come to the field;   65
          If not, when you have stomachs.
                                        Exeunt Octavius, Antony, and army
CASSIUS Why now blow wind, swell billow, and swim bark!
          The storm is up, and all is on the hazard.
BRUTUS Ho, Lucilius, hark, a word with you.
                          Lucilius and Messala stand forth
LUCILIUS   My lord.
                    [*Brutus speaks apart to Lucilius*]
CASSIUS Messala!
MESSALA   What says my general?
CASSIUS   Messala,   70
          This is my birthday, as this very day
          Was Cassius born. Give me thy hand, Messala.
          Be thou my witness that against my will
          (As Pompey was) am I compelled to set
          Upon one battle all our liberties.   75
          You know that I held Epicurus strong
          And his opinion. Now I change my mind
          And partly credit things that do presage.
          Coming from Sardis, on our former ensign
          Two mighty eagles fell, and there they perched,   80
          Gorging and feeding from our soldiers' hands,
          Who to Philippi here consorted us.
          This morning are they fled away and gone,
          And in their steads do ravens, crows, and kites
          Fly o'er our heads and downward look on us   85
          As we were sickly prey. Their shadows seem
          A canopy most fatal under which
          Our army lies, ready to give up the ghost.
MESSALA Believe not so.

Cassius is in high spirits despite the omens. He persuades Brutus to prefer suicide to captivity. They part in friendship and readiness for whatever the future holds.

1 Can you guess who is speaking? (in groups of four)

Talk together about all the differences between Cassius' and Brutus' language that we find in the play: Lines 103–15 of 1.3 are typical of Cassius, and lines 12–21 of 2.1 are typical of Brutus.

Two of you now close your eyes. The other two read aloud lines 92–125, but saying 'who's this' instead of 'Brutus' and 'Cassius'. After the reading, guess who read Cassius, who Brutus. Is it easy to tell which is which at this point?

2 Brutus loses his place in Heaven (in pairs)

Although he is a Roman, Brutus seems in lines 100–07 to be feeling his way towards the Christian doctrine condemning suicide. His words seem prophetic, but after a pause for thought at line 109, he decides to take the noble Roman's way out of defeat.

Talk together about Brutus' pause for thought and go through everything that must have gone through his mind in that moment before he said 'No, Cassius, no'.

3 Inspiring the troops (individually or in pairs)

Compose a 'pep talk' to be delivered just before the battle by one of the four generals. Make sure it is characteristic of that leader. Sum up what the soldiers are fighting for in stirring phrases. There is a famous 'pep talk' in *King Henry V* (3.1) if you need ideas.

4 Farewells (in pairs)

Practise different ways of speaking lines 115–21. Which do you find most effective?

Cato the suicide of Portia's father in his last stand against Caesar in Tunisia was famous, and inspired many to take the same course; for attitudes to suicide see **Suicide**, page 182

prevent/The time of life bring about the end before one's expected life-span
led in triumph (as a humiliated captive)

CASSIUS   I but believe it partly,
          For I am fresh of spirit and resolved   90
          To meet all perils very constantly.
BRUTUS Even so, Lucilius. [*Advancing*]
CASSIUS   Now, most noble Brutus,
          The gods today stand friendly that we may,
          Lovers in peace, lead on our days to age!
          But since the affairs of men rests still incertain,   95
          Let's reason with the worst that may befall.
          If we do lose this battle, then is this
          The very last time we shall speak together.
          What are you then determinèd to do?
BRUTUS Even by the rule of that philosophy   100
          By which I did blame Cato for the death
          Which he did give himself – I know not how,
          But I do find it cowardly and vile,
          For fear of what might fall, so to prevent
          The time of life – arming myself with patience   105
          To stay the providence of some high powers
          That govern us below.
CASSIUS   Then if we lose this battle,
          You are contented to be led in triumph
          Through the streets of Rome?
BRUTUS No, Cassius, no. Think not, thou noble Roman,   110
          That ever Brutus will go bound to Rome:
          He bears too great a mind. But this same day
          Must end that work the Ides of March begun.
          And whether we shall meet again I know not,
          Therefore our everlasting farewell take: 115
          For ever and for ever, farewell, Cassius!
          If we do meet again, why, we shall smile;
          If not, why then this parting was well made.
CASSIUS For ever and for ever, farewell, Brutus!
          If we do meet again, we'll smile indeed;   120
          If not, 'tis true this parting was well made.
BRUTUS Why then, lead on. O, that a man might know
          The end of this day's business ere it come!
          But it sufficeth that the day will end,
          And then the end is known. Come ho, away!   125
                              Exeunt

147

Battle. As Octavius weakens, Brutus orders all troops to attack. On another part of the battlefield, Cassius reports that his soldiers have fled. Flee, says Pindarus, Antony is in our camp.

---

1 'Over now to our reporter at Philippi' (in groups of four)

War reporters on television tell us about:

a what's happening

b the commander's overall strategy

c the state of morale, from general to footsoldier.

Devise a short national news slot about events of Philippi on the opposite page. Use reporters' commentary, newsreel, maps and interviews.

2 Theatre of war (in large groups)

How can the battle be shown and heard on stage? The stage direction 'Alarum' means a loud battle noise made by drums, trumpets, voices and clashing weapons off-stage.

a Start at 5.1.119 and use all resources available to make the sound effects that change scenes up to 5.3.4. Each scene has a different mood and your effects must make this clear. The right volume and quality of noise takes careful planning.

b While some work out sound effects, others work on the staging. Either restrict yourself to the four named characters, or bring on a host of soldiers. Have the whole field of battle in mind when you plot entries and exits. Ensure that you show their contrasting moods: thoughtful, joyful, fearful, dejected, fast, slow or what you feel is appropriate.

All this takes careful organisation, but will tell you a great deal about Shakespeare's stagecraft. You could plan it in the classroom and then act it out in a larger space.

---

bills written orders
cold demeanour in Octavio's wing low spirits in the troops led by Octavius
ensign standard bearer

ACT 5   SCENE 2
The battlefield at Philippi

Alarum. Enter BRUTUS *and Messala*

BRUTUS   Ride, ride, Messala, ride, and give these bills
      Unto the legions on the other side.
               Loud alarum
      Let them set on at once, for I perceive
      But cold demeanour in Octavio's wing,
      And sudden push gives them the overthrow.   5
      Ride, ride, Messala, let them all come down.

                                  Exeunt

ACT 5   SCENE 3
A high place overlooking the battlefield at Philippi

Alarums. Enter CASSIUS *and* TITINIUS

CASSIUS   O, look, Titinius, look, the villains fly!
      Myself have to mine own turned enemy.
      This ensign here of mine was turning back;
      I slew the coward and did take it from him.
TITINIUS   O Cassius, Brutus gave the word too early,   5
      Who, having some advantage on Octavius,
      Took it too eagerly. His soldiers fell to spoil
      Whilst we by Antony are all enclosed.

Enter PINDARUS

PINDARUS   Fly further off, my lord, fly further off!
      Mark Antony is in your tents, my lord,   10
      Fly therefore, noble Cassius, fly far off.
CASSIUS   This hill is far enough. Look, look, Titinius,
      Are those my tents where I perceive the fire?

Titinius leaves, on Cassius' orders. Pindarus reports that Titinius has been captured. Cassius decides on suicide and orders Pindarus to kill him. Pindarus obeys his command.

---

1 Question Marked Innocence (in groups of four)

Here is a poem by a fifteen-year-old who committed suicide at seventeen.

Once . . . he wrote a poem
And he called it 'Chops',
Because that was the name of his
    dog, and
    that's what it was all about.
And the teacher gave him an 'A'
And a gold star.
And his mother hung it on the
    kitchen door,
    and read it to all his aunts . . .

Once . . . he wrote another poem
And he called it 'Question Marked
    Innocence',
Because that was the name of his
    grief, and
    that's what it was all about.
And the professor gave him an 'A'
And a strange and steady look.
And his mother never hung it on the
    kitchen door
    because he never let her see
    it . . .

Once, at 3 a.m. . . . . he tried another
    poem . . .
And he called it absolutely nothing,
    because
    that's what it was all about,
And he gave himself an 'A'
And a slash on each damp wrist,
And hung it on the bathroom door
    because he
    couldn't reach the kitchen.

Talk together about why you think he came to take his life. Can you see any similarities between Cassius' suicide and this boy's suicide?

---

light dismount
in Parthia a campaign in the Iran/
  Iraq area, eleven years before;

Plutarch says Cassius kept
Pindarus 'reserved for such a
pinch', like a cyanide capsule

TITINIUS They are, my lord.

CASSIUS   Titinius, if thou lovest me,
          Mount thou my horse and hide thy spurs in him   15
          Till he have brought thee up to yonder troops
          And here again that I may rest assured
          Whether yond troops are friend or enemy.

TITINIUS I will be here again even with a thought.   *Exit*

CASSIUS Go, Pindarus, get higher on that hill,   20
          My sight was ever thick: regard Titinius
          And tell me what thou not'st about the field.
                    [*Pindarus goes up*]
          This day I breathèd first, time is come round
          And where I did begin there shall I end:
          My life is run his compass. Sirrah, what news?   25

PINDARUS (*Above*) O my lord!

CASSIUS What news?

PINDARUS Titinius is enclosèd round about
          With horsemen that make to him on the spur,
          Yet he spurs on. Now they are almost on him.   30
          Now Titinius – Now some light; O, he lights too.
          He's ta'en.
                    (*Shout*)
          And hark, they shout for joy.

CASSIUS Come down, behold no more.
          O, coward that I am to live so long
          To see my best friend ta'en before my face.   35
                    Pindarus [*descends*]
          Come hither, sirrah.
          In Parthia did I take thee prisoner,
          And then I swore thee, saving of thy life,
          That whatsoever I did bid thee do
          Thou shouldst attempt it. Come now, keep thine oath.   40
          Now be a freeman, and with this good sword,
          That ran through Caesar's bowels, search this bosom.
          Stand not to answer; here, take thou the hilts
          And when my face is covered, as 'tis now,
          Guide thou the sword.
                    [*Pindarus stabs him*]
                              Caesar, thou art revenged   45
          Even with the sword that killed thee.   [*Dies*]

Julius Caesar

Pindarus flees. Messala and Titinius enter with news of Brutus' success over Octavius. They hope to cheer Cassius but find him dead.

1 The end of the Republic (in groups of four or five)

After 500 years the Republic is finished. Like millions of persecuted, defeated, or outlawed people in history – Jews in Nazi Germany, Vietnamese boat people – Republicans anywhere in the Empire realise that life as they knew it is over. Pindarus flees, Messala will fight on, Titinius will kill himself.

a Lines 60–4 are Titinius' lament for the Republic. Take a line each and keep repeating it, building lament like a piece of music. Speaking the verses in any order, start softly and chime your line into the ensemble of voices sparingly, then increase in volume and frequency as grief deepens. Savour the sadness of the words, which reach the listener as a collage of broken phrases.

b Imagine you are a present-day family in your locality. Disaster threatens and you face the same choices: flight, fight or death. You must say goodbye to everything you knew as home: neighbours, shops, streets, your house. The future seems alien and cold, a hostile foreign country whether you leave, stay or die. Improvise your conversation.

2 Error (individually or in groups of three or four)

In Shakespeare's *King Henry IV* Part 2 Rumour is represented by a man with tongues sewn all over his costume. Messala represents Error when he enters wearing a 'wreath of victory' (line 82). At line 67 he tells us how Error was born.

Error is thus a **personification**, presenting ideas or things as if they were human. Elizabethans made long stories out of these abstract personifications. Make up your own story about Error. Perhaps in your story Error could meet Truth.

Design a costume for Error to illustrate your story.

---

apt prone to deception

PINDARUS So I am free, yet would not so have been
          Durst I have done my will. O Cassius,
          Far from this country Pindarus shall run,
          Where never Roman shall take note of him.   [*Exit*]   50

          Enter TITINIUS *and* MESSALA

MESSALA It is but change, Titinius, for Octavius
          Is overthrown by noble Brutus' power,
          As Cassius' legions are by Antony.
TITINIUS These tidings will well comfort Cassius.
MESSALA Where did you leave him?
TITINIUS   All disconsolate,   55
          With Pindarus his bondman, on this hill.
MESSALA Is not that he that lies upon the ground?
TITINIUS He lies not like the living. O my heart!
MESSALA Is not that he?
TITINIUS   No, this was he, Messala,
          But Cassius is no more. O setting sun,   60
          As in thy red rays thou dost sink to night,
          So in his red blood Cassius' day is set.
          The sun of Rome is set. Our day is gone,
          Clouds, dews, and dangers come. Our deeds are done.
          Mistrust of my success hath done this deed.   65
MESSALA Mistrust of good success hath done this deed.
          O hateful error, melancholy's child,
          Why dost thou show to the apt thoughts of men
          The things that are not? O error, soon conceived,
          Thou never com'st unto a happy birth   70
          But kill'st the mother that engendered thee.
TITINIUS What, Pindarus? Where art thou, Pindarus?
MESSALA Seek him, Titinius, whilst I go to meet
          The noble Brutus, thrusting this report
          Into his ears. I may say 'thrusting' it,   75
          For piercing steel and darts envenomèd
          Shall be as welcome to the ears of Brutus
          As tidings of this sight.
TITINIUS   Hie you, Messala,
          And I will seek for Pindarus the while.

                                        [*Exit Messala*]

Titinius places a victory wreath on Cassius' head, then loyally kills himself.
Brutus and others enter and mourn the two dead men. Brutus orders his
fellow Romans to fight on.

1 I am Cassius' sword

Weapons can be objects of reverence and exquisite craftsmanship. In
stories they often have magical powers. Shakespeare's characters
often swear on or by their swords. Cassius introduces us to his
dagger/sword at 1.3.89.

'I know where I will wear this dagger then:
Cassius from bondage will deliver Cassius.'

He stabs Caesar with it (3.1.76) and invites Brutus to kill him with it
(4.3.100). By this scene it has a life of its own: Cassius asks Pindarus
to '*Guide* thou the sword' (line 45) and here it is told to '*find* Titinius'
heart' while Brutus thinks that Caesar wields it 'and turns our swords
/ In our own proper entrails'.

Gather these thoughts into a poem that starts 'I am Cassius'
sword'.

misconstrued misinterpreted
Thasos the island off the coast at
  Philippi

Why didst thou send me forth, brave Cassius?   80
Did I not meet thy friends? And did not they
Put on my brows this wreath of victory
And bid me give it thee? Didst thou not hear their shouts?
Alas, thou hast misconstrued everything.
But hold thee, take this garland on thy brow;   85
Thy Brutus bid me give it thee, and I
Will do his bidding. Brutus, come apace,
And see how I regarded Caius Cassius.
By your leave, gods! – This is a Roman's part.
Come, Cassius' sword, and find Titinius' heart.   *Dies*   90

Alarum. Enter BRUTUS, MESSALA, YOUNG CATO, *Strato, Volumnius,*
and Lucilius, [Labeo, and Flavius]

BRUTUS Where, where, Messala, doth his body lie?
MESSALA Lo yonder, and Titinius mourning it.
BRUTUS Titinius' face is upward.
CATO   He is slain.
BRUTUS O Julius Caesar, thou art mighty yet,
Thy spirit walks abroad and turns our swords   95
In our own proper entrails.
                        Low alarums
CATO   Brave Titinius!
Look whe'er he have not crowned dead Cassius.
BRUTUS Are yet two Romans living such as these?
The last of all the Romans, fare thee well!
It is impossible that ever Rome   100
Should breed thy fellow. Friends, I owe mo tears
To this dead man than you shall see me pay.
I shall find time, Cassius, I shall find time.
Come therefore and to Thasos send his body;
His funerals shall not be in our camp   105
Lest it discomfort us. Lucilius, come,
And come, young Cato, let us to the field.
Labeo and Flavio, set our battles on.
'Tis three o'clock, and, Romans, yet ere night
We shall try fortune in a second fight.   110
                                Exeunt

Battle. Brutus encourages his troops, then leaves. Left behind, Cato is killed in combat and Lucilius (posing as Brutus) captured. Lucilius drops his pretence when Antony enters.

---

1 Swashbucklers (in small groups)

Young men like the one in this picture used to swagger the streets of Elizabethan London. They shouted and banged their swords on their bucklers (little shields) as a general challenge to anyone who wanted a fight. These were the 'swashbucklers'. The authorities thought them a public menace. It is reported that some women found them sexy.

Work lines 4–8 into something like a football chant. Then try it with your own name, and compose your own tag along the lines of 'A foe to tyrants . . .'.

2 Glorious war
(in groups of eight)

This is the only actual fight called for by a stage direction so it must be performed well on stage. Display fighting was a popular entertainment in Elizabethan times.

Plan, in slow motion, how you would stage the fight from *Enter soldiers* to *Young Cato is slain*. Your fight should be convincing, but never dangerous. The golden role of stage-fighting is *safety first*!

3 Brutus' men

Work out what is happening in the scene and what it tells us about Brutus and his men. In particular, think why Lucilius pretends to be Brutus and what he means by line 13 (there are many possibilities).

Plan a staging of the scene to make good sense of every line.

ACT 5 SCENE 4
The battlefield at Philippi

Alarum. Enter BRUTUS, *Messala,* [YOUNG] CATO, LUCILIUS, *and*
Flavius, [Labeo]

BRUTUS Yet, countrymen, O, yet hold up your heads!
> *[Exit with Messala, Flavius, and Labeo]*
CATO What bastard doth not? Who will go with me?
    I will proclaim my name about the field.
    I am the son of Marcus Cato, ho!
    A foe to tyrants, and my country's friend.   5
    I am the son of Marcus Cato, ho!

> *Enter* SOLDIERS *and fight*

LUCILIUS And I am Brutus, Marcus Brutus, I,
    Brutus, my country's friend. Know me for Brutus!
> *[Young Cato is slain]*
    O young and noble Cato, art thou down?
    Why, now thou diest as bravely as Titinius   10
    And mayst be honoured, being Cato's son.
1 SOLDIER Yield, or thou diest.
LUCILIUS   Only I yield to die.
    There is so much that thou wilt kill me straight.
    Kill Brutus and be honoured in his death.
1 SOLDIER We must not. A noble prisoner!   15

> *Enter* ANTONY

2 SOLDIER Room ho! Tell Antony, Brutus is ta'en.
1 SOLDIER I'll tell the news. Here comes the general.
    Brutus is ta'en, Brutus is ta'en, my lord!
ANTONY Where is he?
LUCILIUS Safe, Antony, Brutus is safe enough.   20
    I dare assure thee that no enemy
    Shall ever take alive the noble Brutus.
    The gods defend him from so great a shame!
    When you do find him, or alive or dead,
    He will be found like Brutus, like himself.   25

Antony gives safe custody to Lucilius and sends for word of Brutus. Brutus and followers enter and rest. Separately and secretly he asks them to kill him.

1 Contrasts of war (in large groups)

Scene 4 is violence, glory and action. Scene 5 opens peacefully and quietly. Some dialogue is a whisper, so quiet you can't hear it. Strato falls asleep. But as the voice of battle steadily grows in volume, Brutus' plea for help in his suicide becomes urgent.

Bring out these contrasts by making a tape recording of the script from the start of 5.4 to 5.5.57. Rehearse and co-ordinate sound effects and dialogue very carefully.

2 'Poor remains of friends' (in groups of four or five)

Who are Brutus' 'poor remains of friends'? We have never before seen them in the play. 'Hotseat' each friend. To do this, ask the character all the questions you can think of about who he is. Questions should help a person think of answers, which are made up from imagination and knowledge of the play combined.

You may decide, for example, that your character had an important behind-the-scenes part to play which nobody ever knew about!

Statilius showed . . . came not back Statilius, having got through enemy lines to Brutus' camp, was to show a torch if not many were dead, then return; he showed a torch but did not return

ANTONY This is not Brutus, friend, but, I assure you,
          A prize no less in worth. Keep this man safe,
          Give him all kindness. I had rather have
          Such men my friends than enemies. Go on,
          And see whe'er Brutus be alive or dead,   30
          And bring us word unto Octavius' tent
          How everything is chanced.

                                                    Exeunt

ACT 5   SCENE 5
A rocky place near the battlefield at Philippi

Enter BRUTUS, DARDANIUS, CLITUS, STRATO, and VOLUMNIUS

BRUTUS Come, poor remains of friends, rest on this rock.
CLITUS Statilius showed the torchlight but, my lord,
          He came not back. He is or ta'en or slain.
BRUTUS Sit thee down, Clitus. Slaying is the word,
          It is a deed in fashion. Hark thee, Clitus. [*Whispering*]   5
CLITUS What, I, my lord? No, not for all the world.
BRUTUS Peace then, no words.
CLITUS   I'll rather kill myself.
BRUTUS Hark thee, Dardanius. [*Whispers*]
DARDANIUS   Shall I do such a deed?
CLITUS O Dardanius!
DARDANIUS O Clitus!   10
CLITUS What ill request did Brutus make to thee?
DARDANIUS To kill him, Clitus. Look, he meditates.
CLITUS Now is that noble vessel full of grief,
          That it runs over even at his eyes.
BRUTUS Come hither, good Volumnius, list a word.   15
VOLUMNIUS What says my lord?
BRUTUS   Why, this, Volumnius:
          The ghost of Caesar hath appeared to me
          Two several times by night, at Sardis once
          And this last night here in Philippi fields.
          I know my hour is come.
VOLUMNIUS   Not so, my lord.   20

Volumnius refuses to aid Brutus' suicide. Brutus bids farewell to his friends. He urges them to fly. But he detains Strato, who helps Brutus to take his own life.

1 'Brutus' tongue' (in groups of five)

In taking his own life Brutus is his own biographer. He writes himself a noble death: 'Brutus' tongue / Hath almost ended his life's history'.

Volumnius, an old school friend, disagrees with Brutus twice, but as usual we only hear Brutus' side of the argument. Brutus lies (line 43) to get his uncooperative friends out of the way.

To let Clitus, Dardanius and Volumnius give their point of view, delay Antony's approach and have them refuse to leave. Improvise what happens as they probe the wisdom and sincerity of Brutus' motives both now and in the future. Brutus and Strato defend his actions.

After your improvisation, see if you can read Brutus' part with more conviction and 'realism' than before.

2 Two suicides (in groups of three or four)

Imagine that the accounts of Cassius' death (5.3.1–46) and of Brutus' death (5.5.1–51) are printed side by side in the Roman newspapers.

- Write the newspaper reports.
- As a Roman family, or the clientele of a pub or café, talk over the similarities and differences and compare their nobility.

3 Brutus' death (in pairs)

The picture shows Brutus running on his sword, though in the play Strato holds it. As a mime or tableau, show Brutus' lines 50–1.

beat us to the pit driven us before them (like hunted animals) into a pit – with the implication of a grave

BRUTUS Nay, I am sure it is, Volumnius.
Thou seest the world, Volumnius, how it goes:
Our enemies have beat us to the pit.
                    Low alarums
It is more worthy to leap in ourselves
Than tarry till they push us. Good Volumnius,   25
Thou know'st that we two went to school together;
Even for that our love of old, I prithee
Hold thou my sword-hilts whilst I run on it.
VOLUMNIUS That's not an office for a friend, my lord.
                    Alarum still
CLITUS Fly, fly, my lord, there is no tarrying here.   30
BRUTUS Farewell to you, and you, and you, Volumnius.
Strato, thou hast been all this while asleep:
Farewell to thee too, Strato. Countrymen,
My heart doth joy that yet in all my life
I found no man but he was true to me.   35
I shall have glory by this losing day
More than Octavius and Mark Antony
By this vile conquest shall attain unto.
So fare you well at once, for Brutus' tongue
Hath almost ended his life's history.   40
Night hangs upon mine eyes, my bones would rest,
That have but laboured to attain this hour.
                    Alarum. Cry within, 'Fly, fly, fly!'
CLITUS Fly, my lord, fly!
BRUTUS   Hence! I will follow.
                    [*Exeunt Clitus, Dardanius, and Volumnius*]
I prithee, Strato, stay thou by thy lord.
Thou art a fellow of a good respect,   45
Thy life hath had some smatch of honour in it.
Hold then my sword and turn away thy face,
While I do run upon it. Wilt thou, Strato?
STRATO Give me your hand first. Fare you well, my lord.
BRUTUS Farewell, good Strato.
                    [*Runs on his sword*]
                    Caesar, now be still,   50
I killed not thee with half so good a will.   *Dies*

*To the sound of the retreating conspirators' trumpets, the triumvirs
enter and accept Brutus' followers into their service. Antony honours Brutus
as the only selfless conspirator.*

1 Clemency – wisdom or folly? (in groups of four)

Octavius shows clemency (mercy) to all of Brutus' followers when he
spares their lives. Julius Caesar also showed clemency to the followers
of Pompey after he had defeated them. Among Pompey's followers
were Brutus and Cassius, who assassinated the forgiving Caesar. Is
Octavius making the same mistake as Caesar? Two of you take the
part of Octavius. The others play advisers who are not happy with
Octavius' decision. Debate who is right.

2 Loyalty to dead leaders (in groups of five or six)

Trotskyites and Stalinists are all Communists, but are bitterly divided
against each other. Likewise, among Republicans, Antony's words
about Brutus (lines 68–75) must please Brutus' followers but anger
those of Cassius. Divide yourselves into Brutusites and Cassiusites.
Argue about who should take the blame for the failure of your cause.

3 Roll the credits

Imagine you have just made a film of the play. At the end, you need an
image or series of images over which to roll the credits, with
appropriate music.

- Describe or draw the images.
- Detail the mood of the music (or choose a specific piece which you
  can perhaps play in class).
- Write notes to explain your 'credits'.

---

retreat on drums or trumpets
entertain take into my service

prefer recommend
part share

Alarum. Retreat. Enter ANTONY, OCTAVIUS, MESSALA, LUCILIUS, *and the army*

OCTAVIUS What man is that?

MESSALA My master's man. Strato, where is thy master?

STRATO Free from the bondage you are in, Messala.
    The conquerors can but make a fire of him: 55
    For Brutus only overcame himself,
    And no man else hath honour by his death.

LUCILIUS So Brutus should be found. I thank thee, Brutus,
    That thoū hast proved Lucilius' saying true.

OCTAVIUS All that served Brutus I will entertain them.   60
    Fellow, wilt thou bestow thy time with me?

STRATO Ay, if Messala will prefer me to you.

OCTAVIUS Do so, good Messala.

MESSALA How died my master, Strato?

STRATO I held the sword, and he did run on it.   65

MESSALA Octavius, then take him to follow thee,
    That did the latest service to my master.

ANTONY This was the noblest Roman of them all:
    All the conspirators, save only he,
    Did that they did in envy of great Caesar.   70
    He only, in a general honest thought
    And common good to all, made one of them.
    His life was gentle, and the elements
    So mixed in him that Nature might stand up
    And say to all the world, 'This was a man!'   75

OCTAVIUS According to his virtue let us use him,
    With all respect and rites of burial.
    Within my tent his bones tonight shall lie,
    Most like a soldier, ordered honourably.
    So call the field to rest, and let's away   80
    To part the glories of this happy day.

                                        Exeunt

Julius Caesar – a play for every age

Julius Caesar was probably written in 1599. It is essentially a tragedy, but it is also a history play, the last of ten by Shakespeare. The play is about politics and war but is different from the other history plays because it is not drawn from English history or from Tudor England's recent past.

Yet the feeling that great events are happening, events that will shape all subsequent history, is unmistakably present. This may be ancient history, but it is told with racy vitality. How is this achieved?

Probably by its mixture of old and new. Shakespeare's Rome owes much to Tudor London – its people even dress in doublets – but it is spiced by specifically pre-Christian superstition and cruelty. The pagan world had not yet learned of the teaching of Jesus Christ, though men like Cicero had brought it 'civilisation' and 'culture'.

In his Rome, Shakespeare's debate about authority can be conducted without fear that the Tudor monarchy be libelled or religious controversy aroused. Yet all the important questions are here, relevant in Tudor times and relevant today:

- Who is fit to bear authority?
- Who is fit to take it away?
- Can authority ever be fully justified, whether by legal or divine ordination?
- Can rebellion ever be justified, especially when we count the cost in human suffering?

These questions were to be asked time and again in the forty years after *Julius Caesar* was written, as England moved towards the bloody Civil War that began in 1642.

The illustrations, and the activities that face the script will encourage you to think of *Julius Caesar* as a play not only about Ancient Rome but also Tudor England. Most importantly, it is about the society you live in today. Wherever people live in groups (school classes, families, political parties, governments or super powers), this play will be relevant, because human nature does not fundamentally change. Questions of leadership, of right and wrong, are ever-present.

Brutus, Cassius and Antony are all around us. They may not be in the concentrated form we find them in the play, but their characteristics are found in many different people today.

We cannot escape being modern readers, actors and audiences of the play. But it is easier to get to the heart of *Julius Caesar* if we understand the 'mental furniture' of an educated Elizabethan. Some of that Elizabethan general knowledge is set out in the following pages. It is arranged in alphabetical order so that neither the Ancient nor the Tudor World seems more important. It will help your insight into the play and aid your active work.

An alphabetical miscellany of Roman and Elizabethan fact and fiction

Animals were everywhere in Rome, as in Tudor London. Transport was by horse and donkey. Farm animals were driven down main roads to market. In Rome, animals also had religious uses, so temples were full of them. Most leading Romans owned farms and shared the hard physical work with their slaves, so even senators refer frequently to animals. Collect your own list of animals mentioned in the play.

Antony (83–30 BC) was a soldier with a reputation for womanising and riotous living. He campaigned with Caesar and reached high government office through Caesar's favour. After the events of *Julius Caesar*, he and Octavius campaigned together. He married Octavius' sister but left her to live with Cleopatra, Queen of Egypt. Octavius was furious and fought a successful battle against Antony, who took his own life. Shakespeare's *Antony and Cleopatra* will help you follow Antony's life and death after Philippi.

Armies in Rome as in Tudor London, were privately owned. They were paid for by individuals who sometimes put them at the service of the state. Tudor monarchs made strict rules about the number of retainers their nobles could keep in London. Such 'private armies' were an obvious threat to a ruler's authority. So don't think of a Roman or Tudor army as a national institution. Within their own territory, aristocrats were like monarchs. Write your own account of a soldier serving in Antony's or Brutus' army – or in the service of a great Elizabethan Lord.

Brutus (85–42 BC) came from a distinguished family. His ancestor threw the tyrannous Tarquin royal family out of Rome and established the Roman Republic. Brutus was highly educated, and wrote some books on philosophy. He fought with Pompey against Caesar in the Civil War, but like all Pompey's followers he was pardoned and grew to be respected and trusted by Caesar. Some claim he was Caesar's secret son.

Julius Caesar

Caesar (100–44 BC) rose to his position of absolute power by clever manipulation of influential people. He amassed wealth and popular support during his successful campaigns in Europe, Asia and Africa, much as, in Tudor times, Drake and Raleigh gained power by the fabulous success of their voyages of piracy and exploration. Caesar, Pompey and Crassus, all successful generals, formed the first Triumvirate: three consuls with absolute power over a third of the Empire each, but answerable to the Senate. After the Civil War of 48 BC, when he defeated Pompey, Caesar made himself dictator for life.

The Capitol was the walled part of Ancient Rome. In the map overleaf of London in Shakespeare's day you can see the Tudor walled city in the East. The City was an immensely crowded and busy place, in contrast with the West End, where royalty and aristocracy maintained their spacious palaces and gardens. In spite of its power and influence the West End had to treat the City with respect. That was because royalty and aristocracy relied on the City's money, and feared its tradespeople who could unite and form a mob. Remember, there was no police force or standing army.

Although the Globe Theatre was not built when the map was drawn, you can see two similar round buildings on the South Bank of the Thames. These were Bear Gardens, where bears were tied up and savaged by dogs for sport. They were sometimes used as playhouses. The South Bank was a 'red light' district where Londoners went for entertainment. Play-going and prostitution had a long association. This underlies Caesar's remark that Antony loves plays (1.2.203). The City offered no such pleasures because the puritanical City Fathers would not allow it. City Fathers were known to enforce rules about clothing as Flavius and Murellus do (1.1.2–5).

Find out more about London's South Bank today, especially about the rebuilding of Shakespeare's Globe. Information can be obtained from *The International Shakespeare Globe Centre*, Bear Gardens, Bankside, Liberty of the Clink, Southwark, London SE1 9EB.

Cassius (?–42 BC) fought with Pompey against Caesar and was pardoned, but did not receive Caesar's favour. Historically, he is a shadowy figure.

Cato is a name that stood for die-hard Republicanism (see also **Government**). Cato the Elder, Portia's great great grandfather, was a general and a statesman of exceptional ruthlessness. He opposed all change because it would destroy the 'simple' life of Ancient Rome. He especially despised the 'easy living' which some Romans brought back from Greece. His great grandson, Portia's father, (95–46 BC) fought with Pompey against Caesar in the Civil War, where he took his own life rather than be defeated.

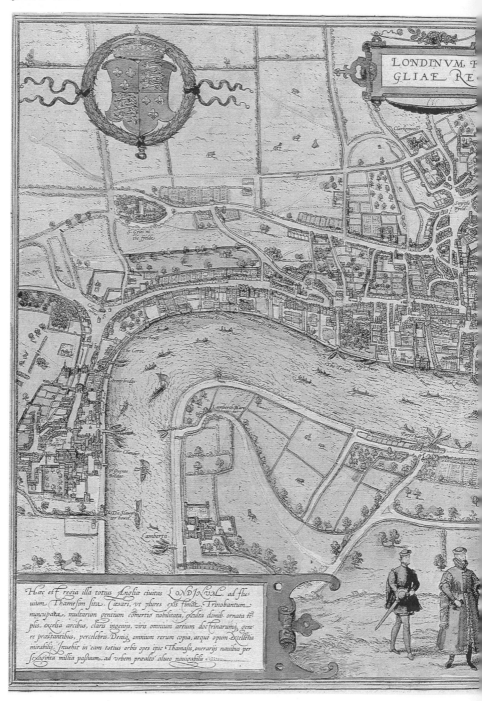

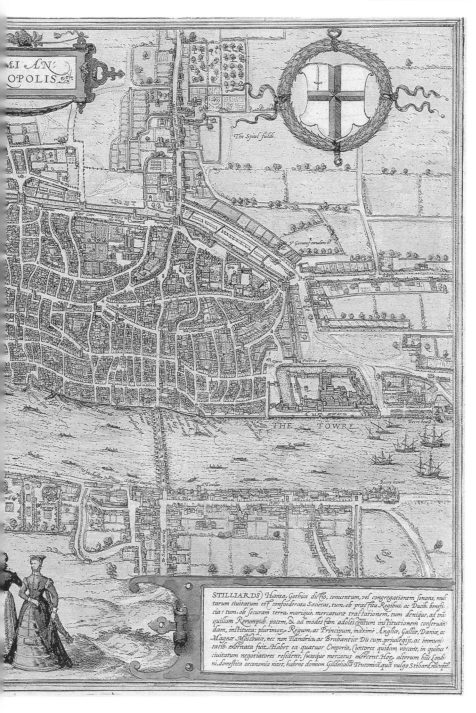

Cicero (106–43 BC) was the leading orator of his day. His writings were intensely studied in Elizabethan schools. His style was held up as the ideal model for all students. His essays, letters and imaginary conversations between well-known historical figures popularised and simplified the ideas of the Greek philosophers, presenting them in a style that was pleasurable and easy to read. Through him, the ideas of the Ancient World became familiar to the people of Renaissance Europe in Shakespeare's time. Turn to the extract from Cicero on page 124 to remind yourself of his style.

Common pulpits outside in public places existed both in Tudor London and Ancient Rome. They were places where you could voice controversial views. St Paul's Cross in the churchyard of St Paul's Cathedral was the scene of many politically disruptive sermons, especially from Puritans. Important news was announced there, such as the Armada Victory.

Government Rome was governed by an elected assembly called the Senate. This meant that the country was owned by the people, not by a king or queen as in a **Monarchy**. The Romans called this system *res publica*, which means 'things for the common good' (that's how we have the word 'Republic'). Rome had been governed in this way for 400 years. The old Republican families of the tiny city state, which controlled a vast Empire, were fiercely proud of their practical, efficient system of government. They despised anything that smacked of the superstition and pomp of monarchy.

But Rome was not a democracy as we would think of it today. Voting power was hugely unequal. Roman citizens were divided into five ranks. Each rank had a number of seats in the Senate. In Caesar's day the Patricians were the top four ranks, even though they were a small proportion of society as a whole. They held 368 out of 373 seats! This meant that the Plebeians, the vast majority of the citizens of Rome, were represented by only five seats. Slaves had no vote at all. People outside Rome, in the rapidly growing Roman Empire, had no say in their government, even though they paid heavy taxes to Rome. The Republic was fast becoming a tyranny, because only the tiny handful of original Roman aristocratic families had any power at all.

Julius Caesar made much use of the people's discontent with the Republic, and he used his huge fortune to find favour with the

Plebeians. Ordinary people saw they had more to gain from him than from the aristocratic families of the Senate. Caesar's military might and influence with the people made him the only person able to maintain order and protect Rome. He was, therefore, elected to the office of Dictator without difficulty. This office, which gave him absolute power, was only meant to be filled as a temporary measure in a time of emergency but Caesar had himself made Dictator for life.

Such a lack of genuine democracy seems shocking to us today, but in Shakespeare's day things were not so very different. Parliament was an elected assembly but only a small proportion of the population had the vote. It only ever met when Queen Elizabeth ran out of money and needed to raise cash.

Honour in ancient times and in Shakespeare's day, honour was not the vague concept it is today. It was the subject of a great ethical debate which will much enrich your study of *Julius Caesar*. A vital starting point is Aristotle's *Nichomachean Ethics*, which defines 'the Good' as it should appear in people's behaviour. Aristotle's section on the **Magnanimous Man** (see below) is his definition of the perfect ruler. All later ancient writers, like Cicero, drew on Aristotle for their discussion of ethics (moral behaviour).

During the **Renaissance**, when writers such as Aristotle were rediscovered, the code of honour came into head-on collision with Christian thinking. The Magnanimous Man's intense *pride*, for example, conflicted with the Christian insistence on *humility*. Writers on ethics struggled to reconcile the two moralities. So the idea of *personal* rather than *public* honour was promoted. This meant that you could know yourself to be a virtuous person even if you were not praised by the world. This is like the Christian idea of conscience.

In duelling, the code of honour was worked out down to the smallest detail. Conduct before and during a duel was a measure of character. In Shakespeare's plays duelling terms are woven into the language. Notice how Caesar (3.1.48) and Brutus (3.1.141) use the word 'satisfied'.

Nowadays, we can get a better understanding of what honour meant to Elizabethans if we think of the Mafia 'man of honour'. Look out for uses of 'honour' today. Collect examples to discover what it means to different groups or nations. Talk together about what 'honour' means to you.

The Lupercal was originally a farming festival held on 15 February to ward wolves off the newborn lambs and kids in the flocks. Later it was adopted by the city of Rome to ward off evil spirits. Young men, dressed only in a girdle of goat skins, 'beat the bounds' of the city. Goat skin was chosen because billy goats are sexually potent and able to fight off the wolves. Just as the billy goats brought fertility to the flocks, so barren women believed the flick of a goat skin flail would enable them to have children (see **Plutarch**).

The Magnanimous Man is described in a translation from Aristotle. As you read it, think how Brutus, Cassius, Caesar and Antony measure up to this perfect standard:

Honour, his chief concern
The Magnanimous Man is chiefly concerned with honours and dishonours. He is moderately pleased with honours conferred on him by good men because he reckons that to be his due (or rather less than his due because no honour can be worthy or perfect virtue – yet he accepts such honours because people have nothing greater to give him). But he utterly despises honours from lightweight people that are given for trivial reasons, because he deserves better than that. He despises dishonours too, because in his case they cannot be just. Power and wealth are only desirable to him for the sake of honour. Even honour is a little thing to him, so everything else must be of even less importance. Consequently people think magnanimous men look down on everybody else.

Courage
The Magnanimous Man does not run into trivial dangers but he will face great dangers. In danger he has no thought for his own life because he knows that there are conditions on which life is not worth having.

Obligations and bearing towards others
He is the kind of man that does things for other people but is ashamed to have things done for him because it puts him in an inferior position. Thus he tends to return an even greater favour than the first, so that he not only repays but puts the other person in a position of obligation to him. The Magnanimous Man asks for nothing but gives help readily. He stands on his dignity with high-class people but is relaxed with those of the middle class, because it is not only easy but bad mannered to be superior with inferior people. It is as bad as a strong person bullying a weak person. But it is a difficult and stately thing to be superior with superior people.

Frankness
Also, he loves and hates openly because it is cowardly to hide your feelings or to care less for truth than for what people will think. He does not care what he says because all people are beneath him, and he always speaks the truth. He admires nothing because nothing to him is great. He never gossips or talks about himself or other people because he would prefer to hear neither good of himself nor bad of other people.

Monarchy in the Christian world takes its authority from the Old Testament in the Bible. Samuel anointed Saul as the first king of the Israelites, touching his head with holy oil, just as monarchs are anointed today. When Christianity became the religion of Europe, kings could only hold authority by the grace of the Lord's representative on Earth, the Pope. This system lasted from about 1000 to 1500. However, during the sixteenth century, the Pope's power was severely challenged by the idea that God's grace was not available exclusively through the Roman Catholic Church. Rulers in Protestant countries 'protested' against the Pope's authority. Elizabeth's father, Henry VIII, broke from Rome because the Pope would not allow him a divorce. But although the break gave the Tudors considerable power, it also called into question the whole basis on which monarchy held its authority. Geneva, the state which Protestants admired as an ideal model of government, was not a monarchy but a Republic. It was governed by a council of stern priests who supervised every aspect of life in the state. In the play, Cassius pours scorn on the idea of monarchy while Antony upholds it.

Monarchy meant power passed from parent to child, authorised by the divine power of the church, whose magnificent ritual, vestments and mystery kept a superstitious people in subjection. Extreme Protestantism (Puritanism) meant the devolution of power to elected assemblies. Puritans were fiercely opposed to anything that smacked of ritual or idolatry. In Elizabethan and Jacobean England, Rome and the Pope were portrayed as the venomous source of all that was deliberately misleading in religion.

Organise a class debate on the statement 'Republics are preferable to Monarchies'. Use evidence from *Julius Caesar*, history, and the modern world to argue your points of view.

Octavius (63 BC–14 AD) was grand nephew to Julius Caesar. He achieved high office at an early age, as his ability was recognised by Caesar, who treated him as his heir. After the events of *Julius Caesar*, he and Antony quarrelled. After defeating Antony in battle, Octavius became sole ruler of the Empire. During his reign, many fine buildings were erected and the arts flourished. He became known as 'Augustus', meaning 'sacred' or 'revered'. In the **Renaissance**, links were made between his beneficent rule and the birth of Christ which took place in his time.

The **Politics of religion** constantly threatened Elizabeth's reign (1558–1603) even though it was one of the most secure that English people had known for hundreds of years. But who would follow her on the throne? Elizabeth had no heir. In 1599, when she was an infirm sixty-six-year-old, people dreaded that only civil and religious strife would settle the question of who was to succeed her.

This illustration is part of a design for an imaginary monument giving thanks for the failure of Roman Catholic plots against England's Protestant Monarchy and its government. At the base, the Pope's crown is shown trampled underfoot with the devil. (But Rome was not the only threat. While Shakespeare was writing *Julius Caesar*, one of Elizabeth's own favourites, the Earl of Essex, rebelled in 1601. He intended to break the power of the queen's Secretary of State, Sir Robert Cecil, and to replace him with a group of young aristocrats. His plot to march with a mob to Westminster failed.)

Far more damaging in the long term to the whole idea of Monarchy were the activities of loyal Puritans. Their insistence on democracy in Church and Parliament was backed by genuine popular feeling and efficient organisation, especially in the City of London. It was from the lips of Puritan radicals like Peter Wentworth or John Field that words like 'liberty, freedom and enfranchisement' (3.1.81) would have been heard in Shakespeare's day.

Research one of the plots against Monarchy during Shakespeare's life.

Plutarch (46–120 AD) was a Greek historian whose *Lives of the Noble Grecians and Romans* was translated into English by Sir Thomas North in 1579. Shakespeare relied almost exclusively on Plutarch for his factual detail. Compare how he presented the events described in these extracts from Plutarch. Work in pairs, one of you reading aloud the Plutarch version, the other reading Shakespeare's.

Compare with 1.2.238–67:

> When they had decreed divers honours for him in the Senate, the Consuls and Praetors accompanied with the whole assembly of the Senate went unto him in the market-place, where he was set by the pulpit for orations, to tell him what honours they had decreed for him in his absence. But he, sitting still in his majesty, disdaining to rise up unto them when they came in, as if they had been private men, answered them that his honours had more need to be cut off than enlarged. This did not only offend the Senate, but the common people also, to see that he should so lightly esteem of the magistrates of the

commonwealth; insomuch as every man that might lawfully go his way departed thence very sorrowfully. Thereupon also Caesar rising departed home to his house, and tearing open his doublet collar, making his neck bare, he cried out aloud to his friends that his throat was ready to offer to any man that would come and cut it. Notwithstanding, it is reported that afterwards, to excuse this folly, he imputed it to his disease, saying that their wits are not perfect which have his disease of the falling evil, when standing of their feet they speak to the common people, but are soon troubled with a trembling of their body and a sudden dimness and giddiness. But that was not true. For he would have risen up to the Senate, but Cornelius Balbus one of his friends (but rather a flatterer) would not let him, saying: 'What, do you remember that you are Caesar, and will you not let them reverence you and do their duties?'

Compare with 1.2 stage direction and lines 1–11 (page 11):

Besides these occasions and offences, there followed also his shame and reproach, abusing the Tribunes of the People in this sort. At that time the feast Lupercalia was celebrated, the which in old time men say was the feast of shepherds or herdmen and is much like unto the feast of the Lycians in Arcadia. But, howsoever it is, that day there are divers noblemen's sons, young men – and some of them magistrates themselves that govern then – which run naked through the city, striking in sport them they meet in their way with leather thongs, hair and all on, to make them give place. And many noblewomen and gentlewomen also go of purpose to stand in their way, and do put forth their hands to be stricken, as scholars hold them out to their schoolmaster to be stricken with the ferula; persuading themselves that, being with child, they shall have good delivery, and also, being barren, that it will make them to conceive with child.

Compare with 1.2 stage directions at line 78 and line 131, then lines 216–44 (pages 15, 19 and 23–8):

Caesar sat to behold that sport upon the pulpit for orations, in a chair of gold, apparelled in triumphing manner. Antonius, who was Consul at that time, was one of them that ran this holy course. So, when he came into the market-place, the people made a lane for him to run at liberty; and he came to Caesar and presented him a diadem wreathed about with laurel. Whereupon there rose a certain cry of rejoicing, not very great, done only by a few appointed for the purpose. But when Caesar refused the diadem, then all the people together made an outcry of joy. Then, Antonius offering it him again, there was a second shout of joy, but yet of a few. But when Caesar refused it again the second time, then all the whole people shouted. Caesar, having made this proof, found that the people did not like of it, and thereupon rose out of his chair, and commanded the crown to be carried into Jupiter in the Capitol.

Pompey (106–48 BC) was, like Caesar, an immensely popular general. He was one of the First Triumvirate with Caesar and Crassus. He cemented the alliance by marriage with Caesar's daughter, Julia. But Caesar made himself immensely more powerful and wealthy by his campaigning in Europe. Pompey stayed in Rome and proved a rather ineffective ruler. So fearful were the Senate of Caesar's power that they forbade him to return to Rome unless he renounced his office of Consul. He agreed as long as Pompey did the same. Pompey refused. Caesar entered Rome and became Dictator three months later. Pompey fled Rome and was finally murdered. *Julius Caesar* opens just after Caesar has wiped out a final pocket of resistance headed by Pompey's sons.

Renaissance is the name given to an intellectual and cultural movement that began in Italy in the fourteenth century. It flourished in Europe until the mid-sixteenth century. It revived the Classical learning, art and architecture of Greece and Rome, and celebrated humanism: the dignity of man.

Sacrifice of animals was an important ritual in Roman religious observance as it was in the Hebrew Old Testament in the Bible. Most Elizabethans would be more familiar with ideas about sacrifice from the Bible, by that time translated into English and well illustrated, than from Roman literature. In this picture, Elijah's sacrifice of a bullock is successful and shows God's favour:

> 'The fire of the Lord fell, and consumed the burnt sacrifice, and
> the wood, and the stones, and the dust, and licked up the water that
> was in the trench.' (1 Kings 18.38)

The skies are home to the heathen gods and Christian God. They were painted on the canopy over the stage of the Globe. *Julius Caesar* makes literal and symbolic use of the skies. Compile a list of references to the weather, times of day, stars and planets.

Suicide was a controversial issue in the Renaissance. The Ancient World regarded it as noble. Christianity condemned it because God must decide our fate, not ourselves, and it shows contempt for His gift of life. Elizabethans celebrated heroic suicidal acts such as that commemorated in Tennyson's *The Ballad of the Revenge*. Turn to the cast-list on page 1 and identify those characters who commit suicide in the play.

Superstition in the opinion of the Greek writer Polybius, was a binding force in Roman society:

> The greatest advantage which the Roman system has over others seems to me to be in their grasp of religious questions. What the rest of the world condemns, I mean superstition, is a cementing force with them. This side of religion has reached such a state of melodramatic pomp with them, both in private and in civic life, that further exaggeration is out of the question . . . I regard it as an instrument of government. . . . Every democracy is fickle, full of irrational passion, anarchical greed and violence. Your only means of holding it together are the fears of the unseen world and suchlike melodramatic show.

Any decision of importance in Rome was referred to the augurers, who had various ways of determining the will of the gods. Look at 2.2 where Caesar's priests read the entrails: a live animal was cut open and its insides studied. The augurers also decided the calendar, which was not fixed, and decided which days were, or were not, auspicious for conducting business. Caesar himself was an augurer. It was a position of great influence. Are there augurers in today's society? Talk together about what you think of those people who claim to foretell the future.

Triumphs in Ancient Rome were public displays of loot and prisoners captured in a successful campaign. In Shakespeare's day a triumph was more like today's Lord Mayor's Show in London, complete with elaborately symbolic floats and arches (as on page 2).

William Shakespeare 1564–1616

1564 Born Stratford-upon-Avon, eldest son of John and Mary Shakespeare.

1582 Married to Anne Hathaway of Shottery, near Stratford.

1583 Daughter, Susanna, born.

1585 Twins, son and daughter, Hamnet and Judith, born.

1592 First mention of Shakespeare in London. Robert Greene, another playwright, described Shakespeare as 'an upstart crow beautified with our feathers . . .'. Greene seems to have been jealous of Shakespeare. He mocked Shakespeare's name, calling him 'the only Shake-scene in the country' (presumably because Shakespeare was writing successful plays).

1595 A shareholder in 'The Lord Chamberlain's Men', an acting company that became extremely popular.

1596 Son Hamnet died, aged 11.
Father, John, granted arms (acknowledged as a gentleman).

1597 Bought New Place, the grandest house in Stratford.

1598 Acted in Ben Jonson's *Every Man in His Humour*.

1599 Globe Theatre opens on Bankside. Performances in the open air.

1601 Father, John, dies.

1603 James I granted Shakespeare's company a royal patent: 'The Lord Chamberlain's Men' became 'The King's Men' and played about twelve performances each year at court.

1607 Daughter, Susanna, marries Dr John Hall.

1608 Mother, Mary, dies.

1609 'The King's Men' begin performing indoors at Blackfriars Theatre.

1610 Probably returned from London to live in Stratford.

1616 Daughter, Judith, marries Thomas Quiney.
Died. Buried in Holy Trinity Church, Stratford-upon-Avon.

The plays and poems
(no one knows exactly when he wrote each play)

1589–1595 *The Two Gentlemen of Verona, The Taming of the Shrew, First, Second and Third Parts of King Henry VI, Titus Andronicus, King Richard III, The Comedy of Errors, Love's Labour's Lost, A Midsummer Night's Dream, Romeo and Juliet, King Richard II* (and the long poems *Venus and Adonis* and *The Rape of Lucrece*).

1596–1599 *King John, The Merchant of Venice, First and Second Parts of King Henry IV, The Merry Wives of Windsor, Much Ado About Nothing, King Henry V, Julius Caesar* (and probably the *Sonnets*).

1600–1605 *As You Like It, Hamlet, Twelfth Night, Troilus and Cressida, Measure for Measure, Othello, All's Well That Ends Well, Timon of Athens, King Lear.*

1606–1611 *Macbeth, Antony and Cleopatra, Pericles, Coriolanus, The Winter's Tale, Cymbeline, The Tempest.*

1613 *King Henry VIII, The Two Noble Kinsmen* (both probably with John Fletcher).

1623 Shakespeare's plays published as a collection (now called the First Folio).

Julius Caesar

Thanks are due to the following for permission to reproduce photographs:

1–2, astronaut: NASA; tickertape: Bettmann Archive; elephants, Romans: from Montegua's *Triumph of Caesar*; 16, Galleria Borghese/Scala; 32, 181, from Hans Holbein the Younger: *Images of the Old Testament*, 1549; 38–9, from Doré's edition of *Paradise Lost*; 52, 160, reproduced by permission of the British Library; 64, 179, Mansell Collection; 72–3, Romans: from Pirelli's *Istoria Romana*; assassination: Topham Picture Source; 74, Bibliotheek der Rijksuniversiteit te Utrecht; 76, 98, Don Cooper; 108, 126, Reg Wilson; 109, 122, reproduced by permission of the Trustees of the British Museum; 110–11, Cassius & Brutus, Brutus reading: from *On Producing Shakespeare* by Ronald Watkins, drawings by Maurice Percival, Michael Joseph Ltd, 1950. By permission; coffins: Photothèque des Musées de la Ville de Paris/Musée Carnavalet, Elizabethan army: from *The Image of Ireland*, 1586, Dummond Collection, Edinburgh University Library; 138–9, Tate Gallery, London; 154, Roget-Viollet; 172–3, The Archbishop of Canterbury and the Trustees of Lambeth Palace Library; 166*l*, Marlon Brando as Antony; 166*r*, from *On Producing Shakespeare* by Ronald Watkins, drawings by Maurice Percival, Michael Joseph Ltd, 1950. By permission; 167, reproduced by permission of the Billy Rose Theatre Collection, N.Y. Public Library at Lincoln Center; Astor, Lenox & Tilden Foundations.

Jacket: Mansell Collection

Thanks are due to the following for permission to reproduce copyright material:

p. 100 Extract from police report of 1888 quoted in *Jack the Ripper: The Final Solution* by Stephen Knight (Harrap, 1976). Reproduced by permission of the Harrap Publishing Group Ltd. p. 124 Extract from *On the Good Life* by Cicero, translated by Michael Grant (Penguin Classics, 1971), translation, introduction and notes copyright © Michael Grant Publications Ltd, 1971. Reproduced by permission of Penguin Books Ltd. p. 150 Poem (page 105) from *Christmas Crackers* selected by John Julius Norwich (Penguin Books, Second Edition, 1982), collection and introduction copyright © John Julius Norwich, 1980. Reproduced by permission of Penguin Books Ltd. p. 178 Extract from *Shakespeare's Plutarch* edited by T. J. B. Spencer (Penguin Books, 1964), copyright © T. J. B. Spencer, 1964. Reproduced by permission of Penguin Books Ltd. p. 182 Extract from *Polybius* from the Macmillan Series of Translations, translated by E. S. Schuckburgh, quoted in *Cicero and the Roman Republic* by F. R. Cowell.